WALKING KHUSH INDIA

====

John A. Massey

Walking Khush India

In Hindi, the word *khush* (**or** खुश) means *happy*

For my wife, Michelle –

you did this to me!

When was the last time you did something for the first time?

John C. Maxwell

Then one day, when you least expect it,

the great adventure finds you.

Ewan McGregor

Contents

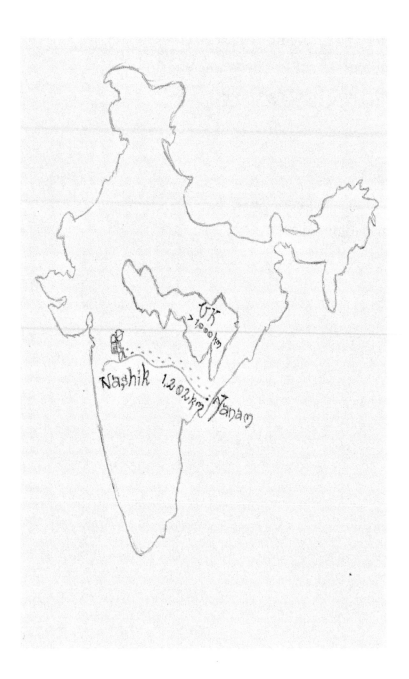

Chapter 1
Shoe-bites

It looked infected and I knew if I wanted to continue any time soon, I would have to burst it.

It was day 4 of my walk across India following the Godavari River and I was struggling. I knew that blisters were going to be something that I would have to deal with, but to be so bad and after only four days, was very worrying. I had read everything I could. Prepared myself with as much help and advice on how to look after my feet and treat blisters when planning a long walk. I couldn't have done any more.

There were so many different approaches that could be taken. It reminded me of reading all those parenting books - those made available to us before our first son was born. In the end, after reading at least six of them, it all came down to common sense.

But somehow, dealing with blisters was a bit more than just common sense; it was physical. Or was it? Did they really hurt when I was walking, or was it my brain playing tricks on me?

Should I simply ignore the pain, and just carry on walking?

====

Before the trip, I had spent some time in Southport, England, with my mother-in-law, Dorothy. I was back in the UK on business and

Dorothy didn't live too far from where I was working and I knew that while I was staying there, I would have time to get all the provisions I needed for my walk. One of these provisions being plasters - and a lot of them.

Dorothy and I walked down the road from her house to a large, well-known supermarket. Dorothy was happy to come to the supermarket with me and was, no doubt, overwhelmed by the idea that her son-in-law had decided to hike across India.

"What do we need here, John?"

"Plasters" I replied with an emphasis on the *ar* sound. I was a Londoner and proud of it. The family I had married into were northerners and the simple pronunciation of this word was more than just a journey along the M6 apart.

"Plassters" she said, correcting me.

"Yes, those sticky things that I hope will prevent me from getting blisters", I said as we entered the shop. We found the medical counter and a kind lady was only too happy to help us. I do find that I'm helped a lot more when I am shopping up north, but maybe it is that everyone up here likes my accent!

"I need some plaaassters" I say. "I think the strip ones that you can cut to size".

"No problem love, how many would you like?" the lady asked as she bent down to see the shelf full of plasters.

"How many do you have?"

She counts, "20 boxes."

"I'll take the lot."

She is on her knees counting out the boxes of plasters and looks up at me. Before I could explain why, Dorothy comes to my rescue: "he needs them; he is walking across India!"

====

I finally saw a hotel, I had been walking for six hours and my feet were telling my brain *really no more*. I was in a small town called Niphad. I have been told it is known for producing the best onions in India. Apparently, it is also known to have a reputation for producing really spicy curries. These facts might have interested me in a previous life, but not now. I was in so much pain I was not eating properly. And I had already lost too much weight in a small space of time.

Being a teacher, most bad situations that can occur in a classroom can be prevented. Well, according to Bill Rogers, a renowned educationalist, it can. If you can sense something is going to go wrong, prevent it from happening. I would like to think that I could use the same principle here from preventing blisters.

Each day before I walked, I needed to spend an hour pampering my feet. Firstly, my boots: they had been nicely worn in before the trip and were made of canvas to allow my feet to breathe.

Secondly, the feet: the slightest "*shoe-bite*" as Indians so happily name blisters, should be given immediate attention. If you can feel a rub, stop and plaster it. Then continue with all the preventions that help and hopefully stop blisters from hampering your progress.

I call these blisters 'stubborn signs'. *Stubborn signs* because I have the feeling they will not be going away any time in the near future. And, *stubborn signs* because it is my determination to keep walking when the feet are telling the brain to stop. I knew I should stop and give these *stubborn signs* all the attention they required, but if I kept stopping every 20 minutes or so, there was no way I was going to be able to walk across this massive country, a distance of over 1000 kilometres.

Plasters go on first where there are any tender patches of skin. Cut to size from the strips and white micro taped to stop them moving. Then the deodorant, followed by talcum powder. Anything that can stop your feet from sweating, the less chance you have of suffering from blisters. If your feet get wet from water or sweat, you need to change your socks. If you don't, your skin gets soft and then the rubbing occurs. Finally, the socks you wear. Well, first you need to wear two pairs to stop the rubbing and obviously your boots need to have enough space to allow this to happen. Through trial and error, I discovered that nylon socks are the best when walking in really hot temperatures.

Before I entered the hotel, my feet were hurting so much that I needed to sit down. The place I had found was just a roadside café, serving simple foods and drinks. I collapsed into a plastic chair, removed my boots and examined the damage. My poor feet were in bits. At least 8 large blisters, four on each foot. One looked really bad after a quick inspection, I thought that it could be infected.

These cafés, restaurants, or shacks, are everywhere along the roadside and had, so far, been a real saviour for me, especially when I needed to buy water. I am drinking sometimes as many as seven litres a day.

This one was really no different from many other shacks I have stopped at. They were constructed as simply and as efficiently as possible. Four to six large bamboo poles were its main support, with a small tin roof, covered with extra blue plastic sheets to give extra shade.

The front of the shop is where the cooking and activities occur: the making of the *chai*, the traditional Indian daily drink, always full of creamy milk and extra sugar; the frying of anything from samosas to dosas. In this part of India, only vegetarian ingredients are deep fried and snacks could be easily purchased without entering the shop.

I ordered a bottle of water and I was just about to re-plaster my feet when some man entered the restaurant. He spoke English and asked why I was here. His name was Rushikesh and we swapped numbers. I explained my mission that I was walking across India for charity. I also gave him a card that was made by one of my teachers in the slum school where I work in Mumbai. This card explained, in Hindi, the reason why some white man, wearing a pink sun hat, would be walking through their neighbourhood. This card would prove to be extremely useful on the trip. After reading this, the locals understood - they were all so supportive and kind. With reference to *Charlie Bucket* from Roald Dahl's famous children's novel, I named this laminated card *"the golden ticket"*.

Rushikesh read it and passed it around the café; soon all the people were approaching me and shaking my hand. Rushikesh then bought me breakfast. We talked and I explained in detail my dream of walking across the whole of India. He told me that about four years ago, he met a Dutch couple in the same café that we are sitting in. He explained that was the first and last time he had ever met any white people, well, until I showed up. He explained that the Dutch couple were on bikes and were only travelling from Mumbai to Nanded. We laughed and I suggested that maybe I should have come by bike; he agreed with me.

"A lot easier, too easy," I say.

"Yes, walking is a lot harder and will take much more time."

Tell me about it, I think, but we just smiled at each other. He then lowered his head to look at my feet which I had rested on another plastic chair, trying to get whatever breeze I could find in this plus 40 degrees heat.

"How far do you have to go?"

"This is my fourth day, maybe another 900 kilometres"
He takes a second look at the underneath of my feet.

"Sorry, my friend, that is not possible with those feet like that," he replied and shook his head.

I looked at him with a sudden realisation that he might be right. The conversation then changed and he talked about how good the local food was in that part of India. Then he got up, paid my bill, shook my hand, and declared that he would keep following my progress. I was just thinking that I needed to get these feet back into my boots and head off for the hotel when the owner of the restaurant came over, bought me chai and a rather tasty cream horn. This simple act of generosity amazed me and I realised how wonderful and giving these people are. I had a feeling that there would be many more similar experiences ahead of me. I thanked him and hobbled to the hotel.

I had never ever needed a hotel so much in my life. The price of the room, the condition of the room, nothing mattered. I need to get to a room and rest my feet. I paid my £5 for the room and, loaded with my heavy rucksack, followed the porter to my room. As luck would have it or not, it was the furthest room away from the reception. Please, I was thinking, any room except this one on the third floor with no lift.

I lay on the bed looking at my blisters. I phoned home and spoke to my friends, Lorraine and Richard. They confirmed what I had already accepted had to be my next move... I would need to burst the blisters. They suggested that once I had done the deed, I would need to soak my feet in salt water. So, another 5-minute walk down to the restaurant to get some salt. Again, my London accent was not understood and the only way I could explain I needed salt was to enter the restaurant and find it myself.

Before the trip, I had made an effort to see a doctor in Mumbai, seeking advice on everything from snake bites, to dehydration and of course, how to deal with blisters. He said never burst a blister.

So I was ready: bucket of salt water next to the bed, and a sharp sterilised needle that sensibly, I had brought with me. I needed to have everything ready close by, because after I had operated, there was no way I could risk walking on the dirty floor until the morning. My reading glasses were on; I needed to be accurate. I began and, ignoring the doctor's advice, I punctured the first blister to release the pus and liquid.

I then thought back to what Rushikesh had said earlier. I really had to be realistic and at this point, I didn't think I had any chance of completing my dream.

Chapter 2
Midlife Crisis

Life just moves on when there is no set routine. I would say it passes slower. I am a self-employed playground consultant and I run my own company and have been doing so for 10 years. I consult primary schools on how to organise their playground. In a typical day, I can teach playground games, including skipping, French skipping and multicultural games to an entire primary school. I am also a qualified primary school teacher and I have been doing that off and on for nearly 20 years.

Being self-employed means that you are totally in control of your time and, if you are lucky, how much money you can earn. Being in control of my work has given me time to share the responsibility of bringing up my two sons: Andrew, 14 and Theo, 12. Being at home has let me watch them grow up, something that a lot of fathers don't have the opportunity to do. My business has allowed me to organise days where I could stay at home, change nappies and later, take the children to and from school. I always shared this responsibility with my wife, Michelle, who is also a primary school teacher. She would work maybe three days a week to allow me to work on the other two. In real terms, we shared one income in order to look after our children.

Children grow up and sadly, no longer need (or want) you to collect them from school ... well maybe only if it's raining! All the time you had set aside to be at home is no longer needed. You find yourself time-rich. This was the time to develop my business. I had no worries about how many days I needed to work; I could work every day. In the past, I had to turn work down due to family commitments, so I thought it wouldn't be a problem getting more work. But it was.

My business is totally reliant on primary schools and the funding they receive pays my wages. There was, and still are, many changes happening in the UK education system, with one of the major changes affecting funding. Schools are now more accountable for how they spend their budgets. In the past, schools had a variety of different budgets, all covering different aspects of school life, all issued by the Local Authority and all monitored by the Local Authority.

Now everything just comes out of one big money pot - the school budget. The funding is looked after under one roof, the school. All monies, including staff wages, resources, books, educational visits, etc. are now the responsibility of the school's finance office or the bursar.
Schools have to decide how to spend their money, whereas previously, they were told by the Local Authority. Within two years, this new system completely wiped out the power of local authorities.

Schools are judged now only by Ofsted and whatever they say dictates where the school directs its funds each academic year. Targets, data and statistics in schools have become more important than the children that attend them. If Maths and English results and targets are the only thing that Ofsted says makes a good school, all funding is pushed into these areas. The service that I supply is play focused and, sadly, this is not included in many schools' budgets.

I tried to go back into the classroom as a supply teacher in Michelle's school; this sort of worked for a bit. But the school soon realised that, due to my years of experience, I was too expensive, and they employed non-qualified teachers to cover the lessons, simply because they are cheaper.

Once again, I find myself with a lot of time on my hands and no extra work. I use my time well and keep the house painted and tidy, but I know this situation couldn't continue forever. 'When and how is this going to change?' was a question I frequently asked myself. The answer came in the shape and form of my wife Michelle.

"John, I am finding it very difficult to continue teaching in this country", Michelle mentioned one day, as she had done nearly every day for the last 5 months.

"It's not why I signed up to become a teacher. I care about the individual child, not about their statistical results. Children aren't statistics".

"I know; I totally agree".

"I have been teaching for nearly 25 years; the school doesn't see me as an asset, an experienced teacher; they see me as a big wage bill. We need to get out".

Time moves on and with no routine and only a small business to run, time goes by slowly. Michelle starts applying for jobs all over the world; this is nothing new. She always does this when she is feeling a bit low.

We have now been happily married for 15 years, and we have been lucky enough to have taught in many different countries all over the world. In fact, we have taught together in the same schools on several occasions and even job shared in New Zealand. We sat down and I thought, 'here we go: this is a pattern that we have experienced before'. We take off to teach somewhere in the world, realise the grass is not greener and return to rural Suffolk. But this time, deep down I knew it was different.

"Before, we have always come back because we knew that we could both teach here, and enjoy life. It is different now. We are not wanted any more in this country as teachers, and our experience is too costly for schools to employ us," she explains.

"That's sad, but you are right; I know it is true".

"Also, I am not getting any younger, and now the children are older, I want to become a headteacher"
"OK, but we can't just take off anywhere in the world. We have the boys to think about. Their sports, their friends and their education"

I didn't think much more of this discussion, but deep down, I knew another move was strongly on the cards. I really didn't want to move again. I made no secret of the fact that I was not keen on the idea. Moving countries, packing up home, re-homing pets, storing cars is not something that can be done quickly. The last time we moved abroad to teach 5 years ago turned out to be a disaster and we were back in the UK earlier than we had planned. So, I was thinking "not again, please". I made Michelle promise that before she started applying for jobs all around the world, she would first ask me and the boys if we could live there.

But Michelle being Michelle, having a strong desire to follow her mid-life crisis, applied for a job in Mumbai, India. I told Michelle that it was not practical to give up the lifestyle we had in the UK and move to one of the most overpopulated cities and countries in the world. I was really not happy that she had agreed to sit the interview. But she went ahead and did the interview and got the job. This was now a big problem.

We don't have many family meetings, but this situation called for one. All four of us, sitting around the dining table in rural Framlingham, Suffolk, UK. We took a vote: stay in Suffolk or move to India? I lost: 3:1 - 3 wanting to go, and me wanting to stay. Followed up by the children saying "what do we have to lose Dad?"

So, this is how I ended up in India. It was my wife's fault.

Chapter 3
Space Is A Premium

So, the move to India was on. A friend kindly agreed to look after the cats; cars were put into storage, (with one being looked after by brother so I could use it when I return from the UK to continue to run my playground business). Furniture was stored and flights were booked. Michelle had to get to Mumbai two weeks before the boys and me, who enjoyed the last two weeks of the summer holiday in Spain without her.

Michelle contacted us from Mumbai, where she was checked into a hotel, before the task of finding more permanent accommodation began. She needed to be at school for the training and being the Headteacher, to make sure all the new staff were comfortable and ready to work.

We said goodbye to friends and family and, after two weeks of fun, myself and my two boys were on the plane, leaving Madrid to fly to Mumbai.

This was not my first time in India. Michelle and I travelled and spent nearly 3 weeks there, 15 years back, on our way to live in New Zealand. Arriving in Mumbai with the boys just brought back that time I spent there in 2003. It was the smell of the spices, mixed with the diesel on the over crowded streets, that transported me right back to India. In a strange way, it was as if I had never been away.

When we travelled here before, we were tourists. This time would be totally different; we were going to be living here. I didn't know how that would feel, only time would tell. Fifteen years ago, we travelled all the tourist sights, seeing the Taj Mahal, Delhi, Jaipur, Varanasi and the Ganges - it was great. I did find trying to exercise a bit of a problem and running on the streets was too dangerous due to the lack of pavements and the sheer volume of traffic. However, I remember finding a quiet street in Mumbai (there can't be many) and running up and down it. Soon I had upwards of twenty children running with me. It was like a scene out of a Rocky film.

But after a few weeks, being your first time, and not being prepared for all India has to offer, it can be a difficult country to travel. I had read before our first visit that India is a place that gets under your skin, I really didn't know what that meant, as travel guides do like to over exaggerate a bit. The travel guide also said it would be a place that you either loved or hated. Years ago, after being conned and cheated on several occasions, Michelle and I were sitting on the plane, happily waving this country goodbye. We both looked out of the window and said in a tired voice, 'good riddance'.

Two days later, when we were travelling through another country, I don't where the question came from but I asked it anyway:

'Michelle, do you miss India?'

"Oh, yes, so much,' was her reply.
I miss it too'.

Both of us understood what the travel guide was trying to say. It also declared that if you are lucky, no one ever visits India once. The guide was right again, and here I was on my second visit.

The timing of our arrival was not perfect; it was the monsoon season. When we were met at the airport by Michelle and a personal driver from the school, the rain was the first thing we noticed. The other thing different was that Michelle was calling everyone '*sir*' and '*maam*', which I thought really odd, but it wasn't long before I was doing the same.

We arrived at the hotel, and soon found ourselves shopping for umbrellas and sweat flannels. It was an important time in India; it was the *Ganesh* festival and the celebrations were evident on the streets. We checked into the hotel and later, even suffering from the effects of jet lag, found ourselves dancing to loud drums, and joining in the festival fun.

I had decided not to work at Michelle's school; I was given the option to either be a classroom teacher or a PE teacher, but I turned both offers down. I had decided that as I would be going back to the UK once a term to continue to run my playground business, I couldn't give the school my full commitment. Again, this left me with a lot of time on my hands whilst the family were at school. I had decided to do some volunteer work, feeling it was time to give something back. Back in the UK, I had contacted an organisation that helped children living in the slum areas of Mumbai. I wanted to be part of that.

The organisation works on the principle that many children in poor areas do not go to school. They provide schooling for these children - either teaching directly in the slums (in rented rooms) or sending a 'teaching bus' for the children to physically get aboard to learn. The children that do not attend school usually only do so for financial reasons; they cannot afford to. Many children from the age of 5 are, sadly, forced to work on the streets or rubbish heaps, collecting plastic bottles or cans or newspapers, anything they can make a few rupees from and their small income is part of the entire family's income giving each family just enough money to eat.

I wanted to help, and when I knew I was moving to India, this is what had kept me motivated. I wanted be a volunteer teacher and work in a Mumbai slum.

With such a new teaching experience, I resolved to keep a diary and this writing, on top of the volunteer work, would fill my time. I decided not to work more than two or three days a week. The rest of the time, when I was not teaching or writing, I would explore my new surroundings.

Just like fifteen years ago when I had first visit Mumbai, I found it difficult to find anywhere to run or exercise. As I said before, the previous time I had managed to find a quiet street to run in, but this time living in an eastern suburb, it wasn't easy to find space anywhere.

I asked the hotel staff if there was any where I could run nearby where I would not get killed by traffic. And, believe it or not, I was offered the roof of the hotel. On my days off, I explored this opportunity and being about 30 metres squared, after ten minutes of running around such a small space, I really didn't feel that this was the answer. Being monsoon season, the ceramic roof tiles were slippery, making running unsafe.

One day with Michelle at school training and the boys not yet having begun the academic year, it was just the three of us, in the hotel. Being an active family, we were always outdoors, running, walking, swimming, on our bikes and exploring. Living here in Mumbai, we knew that that sort of lifestyle would not be possible and that made us sad.

'What are we going to do today?' they asked.

'Get outside and find somewhere we can run,' I answered.

'But it is raining, really heavy'.

'That more than heavy, that's a monsoon,' I laughed.

'So where are we going to run, we can't run on the streets and there are no parks?'
I looked over and opposite the hotel, there was a building site or, as I saw it, some space. Being the middle of a monsoon, there was no-one working - could this be our playground for the day? After all I am a playground consultant. So, putting health and safety to one side, we ventured over.

I checked the area for any real dangers such as open manhole covers, bricks, wires etc. Then I organised a running exercise, with the rain hitting us so hard in our faces we could hardly see. We loved it, and we got to run in a monsoon. But I knew I would need to find somewhere else to exercise if we were going to be able to stay sane in this country.

Days passed and the monsoon continued, I still was trying to run either on the hotel roof or on the building site. I kept looking for a place nearby where I could safely exercise.

Namdev, a helpful waiter at the hotel, suggested I tried a place called *Ghandi Maiden*, and after catching a rickshaw there one day, I knew I had found the place. It was an open park, made from sand and gravel, open 24 hours a day, for all the people in the community to enjoy. At last, I could run, and when I was not teaching, I would go there most days and simply run around the perimeter of the space. Families and young children would be playing cricket, so I had to avoid balls coming from every direction whilst I was running, but at least I had found somewhere I could exercise. It made me feel so much better. The boys would join me there after school and at the weekends where they would join in with the locals, playing either cricket or football, while I just kept on running.

It was in this place whilst I was running that I started to do some serious thinking. I was thinking about why there were not more places like this here in Mumbai? The answer was down to finance. Any spare piece of land in Mumbai, like most large cities, was being bought up by developers for real estate.

If someone owns land, they sell it to build houses: this makes money; parks and open spaces do not make money. Someone told me that Mumbai was the worst city in the world for the lack of available free open space for its people to use. After living here, I would agree. It is so sad.

Having no safe space to exercise and play sport, the children simply do not exercise or play, unless their parents have the money to pay for an expensive coaching club. Poorer people, including their children, do not exercise for fun, and when they saw me running during a monsoon or in 45-degree heat, they could not understand why I was doing it and, understandably, thought I was mad!

As I was running around this park, *Ghandi Maiden*, it made me think of all the luxuries of space that I had taken for granted. In the UK, this was something I had never really considered before. I was lucky enough to live in a place where I could walk down to the local shops and pubs, walk on open fields and parks. I was even lucky enough to be able to walk in a forest and on a beach. But by moving to Mumbai, all this was stripped away from me, and I didn't like it. I think every human being should be allowed the natural freedom of being able to walk, without the risk of being killed by traffic.

I wanted people that do have this natural freedom to enjoy it, cherish it and appreciate it more. For me, running, exercise and walking takes away the stress, leaving me with a feeling of inner peace. I do most of my best thinking when I am running or walking.

What could I do about this situation? I have struggled to find anywhere to run, and I don't think that is fair. I need more people to appreciate the wonders of walking and running. What better way to show its importance than to plan a long walk? Born here, the dream began; to think about the feasibility of walking across India.

Looking back, it was then, at that moment that I decided that I was going to walk across India, unplanned and unguided.

I just hadn't told anyone yet.

Chapter 4
Getting Ready

The dream quickly began to escalate into a reality. I ran more in the mid-day Indian sun, avoiding the monsoon, thinking more and more about how I could possibly make this dream come true. In the early stages, when it was even less than a dream, I told no one. I really needed to think about it, study the map, and see first where I was going to go. Secondly, I needed to think *how* I could do this. I realised if I starting telling people that I was planning to walk across India, they would think I was insane, but more importantly, if I told everyone my plan, and then realised that I had bitten off more than I could chew, it would simply make me look stupid.

I kept a secret between me and myself. It did feel sort of strange, thinking about this journey and not sharing it with anyone else; it's not the way I usually operate. If I have an idea, I like to get people's opinions, then go away and make a judgement having spoken to as many different people has I can. I especially like to talk to my wife Michelle, who always has a different take on an idea, and together we usually come up with the correct solution. But this was an odd situation - the last person I could talk to over this mad idea with was my wife. She would be very worried and concerned and would question my reasons for attempting such a feat. She would then try to discourage me and put me off of this idea before I had even started thinking about how it could be achieved. I knew I would have to secretly plan a route, then, when everything had been finalised, I would tell her. Not having discussed this with my wife, I felt almost afraid to mention this to anyone else, just in case she found out second hand.

My first line of inquiry was of course the internet. I Googled to see if anyone had ever attempted such a feat before. I found that many people had done lots of walking in, and across India before. I was expecting this - India is a magical, mystical place, and many people have enjoyed walking in India before me. Many pilgrimages have taken place, occasions where people have joined together and walked to special temples, or followed a specific religious path.

I wanted to be different. I wanted to try to attempt something no-one had attempted before. I looked at the map, and thought straight away that if I was to do this, I would attempt to walk the largest part of the country. So, if you image India as an inverted triangle, I wanted to walk where the two points were the furthest apart. I wanted to walk right across the middle.

I discovered that some people had walked across India following a river before. People had walked following the River Kaveri in Kerala. People had even walked the whole length of the country following the holy River Ganges. This gave me an idea, and after just finishing Lev King's book, '*Walking the Nile*', I thought maybe I could follow a river too. When I studied the map closely, almost as if it was waiting to be discovered, there it was - the Godavari River - stretching the full width of the country. It was decided then - this would be the river that I would be following. It was the second largest river in India and also the widest. I was excited. I had a plan and I had river to follow across this vast country.

The Godavari River, one of the largest rivers in Indi, is second only to the most famous of Indian rivers, The River Ganges. The main difference between The Ganges and The Godavari is that the Ganges flows north to south the length of the country and the Godavari

flows west to east, the width of the country. In total, the length of
the Godavari River is 1465 kilometres (910 miles), with its drainage
basin covering an area of 313,000 square kilometres (121,000
square miles). At its widest point, it is 583 kilometres across, with a
maximum depth of 40 metres. The river begins in the district of
Maharashtra, near Nashik, 50 miles from the west Coast of India in
the Arabian Sea, and finishes in the Bay of Bengal on the east Coast
of India in Yanam, Puducherry, in the district of Andhra Pradesh.
As with many rivers in India, the Godavari is sacred, and numerous
temples are situated along its banks. [1]

Over the coming weeks, I studied the river. I wasn't too bothered at
this stage about its route; I was more interested in its history. I was
also concerned that someone else may have attempted to walk this
in the past. No one had (and I would find out later why). I was
excited. Could I be the first person to ever walk the whole of India
following this amazing river?

Looking in more detail at the river, it was evident that it was not
only a life line to many people who used its power in the form of
dams to power their electricity. It was more that. It provided food,
water and transport. It also had a very powerful cultural and
religious history and I was fascinated by all the Hindu temples that
were scattered along its banks. For centuries, people had taken
pilgrimages to these sacred places but no-one had walked from its
source to sea. This was my dream, and the fire burning inside me
urged me on, thinking that I could be the first.

I still had not told anyone but I knew, as each day passed, that this
was becoming more of a reality and I would be setting off on this

journey. After getting carried away by being the first person to try such a feat, I had to consider a time scale. I was travelling back and forth to England to run my business, so it had to be a time that I could fit it around my already confirmed diary dates. I worked out the mileage and I worked out that it would be about 1000-1200 kilometres, perhaps longer depending on the route I would take. I figured that if I could manage to walk about 25-30 kilometres a day, I would complete the walk within 60 days. It was at this time I briefly thought about hiring a guide to help me, someone who knew the terrain and the culture, but I soon realised that no one in India would ever dream of walking such a distance and finding a guide could prove to be harder than completing the walk itself. So unguided it would be.

A few weeks passed and I was tempted to plan a route. But something stopped me from doing this. I realised that whatever route I planned out, I may end up changing it all the time, due to all sorts of hurdles that might come my way when I started to walk. So, I thought 'let's attempt this unplanned'. So, there it was: a walk across India, unguided and unplanned. But that was not where the madness stopped. I knew that if I was going to get anywhere near achieving my dream, I needed to be prepared.

Preparation is so important. I knew I would be alone and I really had no idea what route I would be taking, but that didn't mean that I was going to go into this unprepared. Preparations started as soon I had made the commitment to myself. I started searching the net for all sorts of things I thought I would need for this walk. Blisters and how to deal with them, being my largest priority. Then a tent, walking poles, mosquito net, torch - the list just kept expanding. I realised that I could not easily buy all these things here in India, but when I returned to the UK to work, I could come back with all the equipment on my list.

Time was spent looking at my secret list, adding on and taking off things that I thought I might need, then deciding perhaps they may not be needed after all. To be prepared totally I had to know all the finer details: primarily, the length of specific walking time and the date I was planning to set off. I looked closely at my diary and the last time I would be back in the UK would be mid-March. The only time I would have to do this walk would be when I returned from this trip and I would need to have it completed by the end of May, just in time for the start of the Football World Cup, and also in time for when the family finished school for the year. Thinking about getting back for the World Cup would definitely keep me motivated.

Things were slowly slotting into place. I had a destination, a time frame, and a start date. Deciding to start the walk in the new tax year, I planned to leave on the 6th April 2018. One factor that I hadn't really considered was the weather or the temperature. Regardless of what weather was like at this time, this was the only time I could do this walk. Just my luck - this was mid-summer in India and central India would be at its hottest, with temperatures reaching as high as 50°C. I didn't really let this heat fact bother me too much - I just continued with my preparations.

It was getting closer and closer to the time I was leaving India to go back to the UK, so before I left, I knew at some time I would have to tell my wife and family what I had been planning in my head for last the few months.

Sometimes you can plan a moment and then just come out with what you have to say. This was a big deal. I knew that Michelle would be really worried about me, and wouldn't want me to go. So, the timing of breaking the news was all important. Circumstances often have a hand in when you deliver information and I couldn't hold it back any longer. It was one of those forced situations when I knew I had to voice my intentions then.

A normal evening, the children having gone to bed, and Michelle and I were just sitting on the sofa, talking and half watching the television. Michelle just mentioned that because she was teaching French at her school, there was an up-coming French trip and she might have to accompany the students to Paris. I inquired when the trip was going take place and she her reply was 'sometime in April'. The same time I had planned my walk. I knew I had to tell her then. I am never the person for a serious chat, and I was just about to spill the beans, when Andrew came in from his bedroom complaining about a mosquito bite that was infected and was stopping him sleeping. I had already begun the conversation about the French Trip possibly being a problem, as I may not be around at that time, but I had not got around to telling Michelle the reason why. With Andrew's interruption, as she went off to deal with the bite, I told her that we needed to speak.

In Michelle's mind, I know she was thinking 'oh no'. She quickly dealt with the bite and then came back to the sofa looking the most worried I had seen her looking in years.

'What is it John? Are you having an affair? Have you met someone else?'

I was a bit taken aback and shocked by her saying that, and I quickly reassured it that it was nothing like that. She was almost crying, and after my reply, her eyes filled with relief. While she was dealing with Andrew that was all she must have been thinking about. She then looked at me, and said 'are you ill?'

'No'.

So, amongst the tears of relief, the questions came: what do you need to talk to me about? Where are you going in April that will not allow me to go to France?

'Well you know I have been doing a lot of thinking about raising some money for the children in the slum school'.

'Yes'.

'Well yesterday, I reconnected with Matt Bayfield on *Facebook*'. (Matt was an old friend of ours from Framlingham who, sadly, had recently been diagnosed with a malignant brain tumour).

'Sorry, what are you talking about John? Why does Matt Bayfield have anything to do with you wanting to talk to me and you not being here in April?'

'I looked at his blog, and before he was in the wheelchair, he organised lots of walks in the countryside, to raise awareness of his condition and money for the Brain Tumour Charity. People just got together and walked and talked. I saw him being interviewed when he won an award for his efforts in raising money for the charity.'

'Yeah, I remember all the people walking around Framlingham', Michelle interrupted.

'Anyway, he said, whilst he was being interviewed, "just walk". He said "if you can still walk, do it, enjoy that simple pleasure".

'John, where is this going? I am so happy you are not having an affair, but you are making no sense what so ever.'

'Well, the reason you won't be able to go on the French Trip with your students is because I am planning to walk across India.'

So, there it was - out in the open.

Michelle looked at me, doubting my sanity. But after being married for fifteen years, she looked me in the eye and knew I was not joking and that I would do it.

Millions of questions followed over the next few months. Like: couldn't there be an easier way to raise money? Perhaps you should walk a smaller route, or think of another way that wouldn't mean you were so long away from the family.

But it was a burning desire that had to be fulfilled, and once I had committed to it, I was my hardest, strictest boss and if I didn't attempt to start this walk, I would be failing myself. In many ways, letting yourself down can be worse than letting someone else down.

Chapter 5
Talking The Talk

The fundraising began. First, I approached the organisation that I was teaching voluntarily for at the slum. '*Door Step Schools*,' a self-funded organisation that since 1968 has been bringing schools to the doorsteps of children that, due to poverty, did not attend school.

I met with the director of the organisation. I just wanted their support and backing, for I was doing the walk across India to raise funds for their children I was teaching in the slum. I had never really done much fundraising before and I decided I was going to keep it low key. It was mainly the time factor that stopped me making this a world-wide effort to raise money. I was not registered as a charity, and this made it difficult to advertise. I figured if I just used social media, I would hopefully raise enough money to be able to provide at least a phonics reading scheme to the slum children that I taught. The director of *Door Step Schools* was very pleasant and fully supported my idea. However, she was a bit taken aback when I said I would be raising the money as an individual and whatever funds I raised, I would personally be buying and delivering the school books to the slum. It wasn't that I didn't trust the charity. I just wanted to make sure that all the money raised went exactly where I wanted it to go.

Next, I contacted my friend Matt Bayfield and he put me in touch with the Brain Tumour Charity. Again, I explained that I would be collecting the money personally and whatever I raised, I would pass in onto Matt, who has raised a lot of money for the Charity in the past.

With help from my good friend Richard, we set up a *PayPal* account for any friends that wanted to donate to either of the two charities I was collecting for. I could have so easily got carried away harassing people to donate money to my walk, but that somehow didn't feel right. I just advertised through social media and then concentrated more on the act of the walk, rather that the money.

If truth be known, I would have done the walk without raising money, just to make people aware the benefits of walking, and for my own selfish pride. But later on, during the walk, knowing I was raising money for the slum children, and seeing their smiling faces in my head, kept me motivated.

Matt had continued to plug my cause and it wasn't long before I was in talks with Radio Suffolk, who were asking when could they interview me. The local newspaper also heard of my planned expedition and wanted to meet up as well.

Arriving back in England for my playground work in March, I needed to make sure I bought all the equipment for the walk.

The media was on my back. I had fame at last; everyone wanted to interview me and ask me why I had planned to walk across India. Temperatures were down to -5°C and there I was, standing in front of Framlingham Castle (my home town), wearing my logoed *Playground Playtimes* T-shirt (any chance of some free advertisement for my business could only help!), having my photograph taken for the East Anglia newspaper. I was trying to look cool, but I was more than cool, I was freezing. After coming from India, I was literally shivering! This picture was then shared across social media, leading to BBC Radio Suffolk inviting me in for an interview. I thought to myself why not; get more free advertising for my company, and more people hopefully prepared to pay into both the charities I was supporting.

Trying to organise a day when I was not working to find time to be interviewed was difficult. I arranged a date to be live on the Lesley Dolhin show on BBC Radio Suffolk. It had been a long time since anyone had wanted to interview me, the last time was when I was playing football as a teenager, when I once thought I could make the big time and become a professional football player. That was not to be, but being interviewed live was not something that I was used to.

Arriving early at the radio station, I managed to get a reserved parking place for my car. Even this made me feel I was important. I had taken notes; I had told myself to keep the interview simple and clearly state why I was doing this walk and why, and what charities I was raising money for. Oh yeah, of course, mention the family and plug the business.

All went well, and Leslie, the show's host, made me feel so relaxed that before I knew it, I was talking about all sorts of things, some related to the walk, others about my past, which I didn't expect. Even the first time I kissed a girl, most embarrassing!

I left the radio station feeling pleased with the way it had gone and people were phoning me up, congratulating me on the interview and wanting to sponsor my cause. I felt famous, and really quiet enjoyed the spotlight. Now I had a more determined mind set. I had been interviewed and my picture featured in the newspaper. I knew now that I had to follow through with my crazy idea. I had people saying, 'well John if you were thinking of pulling out, you can't now,' and 'do you realise that what you have planned is impossible?' I knew the hardest thing was to tell my family, which I had already done, but now the whole world knew. I had to go ahead with the walk whatever happened, however difficult it might turn out to be. I couldn't let everyone down, the money was coming in quick and fast, all that was left was to walk.

I had talked the talk, now I had to walk the walk.

Framlingham man, John Massey, will be trekking across India for charity.

Picture: Gregg Brown, East Anglia Daily Times 24-02-2018 [1]

Chapter 6
And He's Off!

The equipment was collected and waiting to be packed. I spent a week's holiday with the family in Goa. This is where I decided to buy what would become my instantly recognisable hat. Deciding that a wide brimmed hat would be an essential part of my walking wardrobe, the colour choice can really only be described as madness. I had decided that I would try to find a pink hat; a lady's hat. I figured that if I was mad enough to attempt this journey, I might as well look mad as well.

The search began, and being in Goa, a prime holiday destination, I had many to choose from. Michelle was trying to discourage me from wearing such a stupid hat, asking why I wanted to look that ridiculous. I thought to myself that I was going to look ridiculous whatever I was wearing, struggling with all my baggage across India, what difference would a silly hat make? I was determined to get what I wanted and I found just the hat to accompany me on my walk. A few days earlier, whilst walking to a bar, I spotted the hat I wanted. When everyone was on the beach, I took a walk down to the stall and haggled for the hat. It was big and pink, wide brimmed, definitely female, with a black bow around the crown. It was just the part. When I tried it on, I looked like a cross between my dear mother and Dame Edna Everage.

Two days before I was to set off, I fixed up the tent that I had bought in Spain. I laid everything I thought I needed on the bed: medical equipment, clothes, sleeping sheets, torch, phones, battery chargers, satnav - the list of things I had collected over the month just filled the bed. Someone had advised me that if you are going on a trip where you have to carry everything the whole way, first lay the things on the bed that you think you need and then only take 20% of it. He was so right, but that was not easy. I looked at all the gear and figured that I needed it all. There was no way I could even get rid of 25% of it, let alone 80%.

Trying to pack all I needed took over 2 hours. I quickly realised I did have far too much paraphernalia, so I tried to sacrifice what I could. Eventually I was ready to see if one, my ruck sack could fit it all, but more importantly, two, could I lift it? The tent and walking poles were strapped to the outside of the rucksack (because I had no space left in the rucksack). For a moment, I thought about buying a bigger rucksack, but I knew the smaller the rucksack, the less gear and the lighter it would be for me to carry six hours every day.

Wearing the pink hat and the T-shirt I had had specially printed in the UK, advertising my walk, my business and the charities I was raising money for, the moment of truth had arrived.

I was alone when I first tempted to lift my rucksack and put it on my back to see how it felt. It was a good job I was. If Michelle and the boys had seen what a struggle it was just to lift it - not even managing to carry it - they would have been concerned. I could just about get it strapped around me and walk out of the door of the apartment. I had to reduce it still further, but it was still the heaviest bag I had lifted for years; heavier than any suitcase I have ever packed. I was worried about the weight and had no real idea how I would be able to carry this load all the way across India.

The family returned from school and saw me all dressed up in my walking gear, ready to go. The hat made the boys laugh, but when they saw the rucksack, they just looked at me as if to say 'no way'. Theo, my youngest, who was a strong 10 year old boy, struggled to lift the rucksack off of the floor.

I didn't want to think about the weight and the physical challenge, so I decided I would approach this weight problem when I was walking. I had so much going on inside my head that the physical side of things had been pushed aside. I thought I could deal with that when I was walking. It was naive to think that way, but looking back on it, if I had studied in great detail how tough this walk could be, it might have turned me off and I might never have set off to do it in the first place.

The day came: April 6, time to go. I was up early and said good bye to the family, and I didn't exactly know when I would see them next. We all hugged and cried, and then I left.

Robert was a driver I had met during our stay in Mumbai. I had organised for him to drive me to Nashik, and from there, I would walk to the source the River Godavardi. Then, the next day, just follow the river all the way across India. Easy, eh? Robert was on time and the journey time from Mumbai to the source of the river took about four hours.

We talked and he showed real concern about what I was attempting to do, unplanned and unguided. He spoke good English and he sort of understood why I was attempting this. Leaving the busy city of Mumbai, I got a sense of just how barren this country was.

All the traffic and smog had disappeared and there was countryside all around us. We passed through agricultural land, farming wheat and industrial factories making bricks. Other than the odd person, the only sign of life was the road we were travelling on. I had no idea what the landscape would be like when I was walking but sitting in the car, I could guess. I spoke to Robert and he explained that the route that I was planning to take would be even less populated than what we were passing in the car.

I had not wanted to look on Google to see what I should expect; I wanted to enter into the unknown. That is not that easy in today's world, with instant knowledge available at our finger tips. I wanted to be like an old explorer, I wanted to feel and touch the unfamiliar. Sitting there in Robert's car was my first insight into the Indian countryside where I would be spending all my time over who knows how long. I was excited.

Robert's concerns focused on my safety. I had met him no more than four times previously; he had been recommended to show my family and other English guests around the sights of Mumbai. But we had built up a trusting friendship and what I liked about him was that he was always on time and had never let us down. So, when he spoke, I knew he was speaking the truth and he showed general concern. Did he think I was mad? The answer would most certainly have been yes, but he was more amazed that I was attempting this trip with no real plan and no company.

I got a bit confused when he starting talking, saying that what I was doing was dangerous, and I should not attempt it on my own. I was intrigued, as I felt India was a safe country and I had no worries about being robbed or mugged. My experience showed that India would be amongst one of the safest countries in the world to walk through alone.

I would never attempt such a large walk alone in Africa, South America or maybe even the UK.

'It's not the fear of being robbed you should be worrying about,' he said.

'What is it then?'

'Have you got protection?'

At this point, I did think about making a bad joke. I did not think I would be meeting any women and I am happily married, but thought it would be lost in translation, and he probably wouldn't find it funny anyway. So what protection was needed?

Robert explained that where I was planning on walking, there were wild animals and being alone I could get attacked. He then went on talking about the poisonous snakes and those that could kill you. He thought I would need more than a knife to keep me safe when I am alone.

I had not been so naive that I hadn't studied the snakes to look out for. In fact, India is home to some 270 species of snakes, with 60 being highly venomous. Whilst 1 million people are bitten by snakes every year, only 1-20 people die every year from a snake bite.

Of all of these snakes, there are four snakes that could possibly kill me. The King Cobra; the Krait; the Russell's Viper and the Saw Scaled Viper.

The King Cobra is largest poisonous snake in the world. It has enough venom to kill a large elephant. Once the poison gets into your blood stream, it breaks down tissue and blood cells leaving you paralysed.

With the Krait, its venom hits your respiration system and if untreated, can kill within 4-5 hours.

The Russell's Viper holds the record for the most deaths in India.

The Saw Scaled Viper is the smallest of the main four, but just like the Russell's Viper, this snake is responsible for most of the deaths throughout the Middle- East and Central Asia.

I found out that if bitten by a snake, the best treatment is to get to a hospital as fast as you can. Finding out, or at least knowing what snake has bitten you gives you a better chance of surviving and saves time when receiving the correct anti venom, thus hopefully saving your life. [2]

I had gone to see the doctor before I left, just to make sure that what I was attempting to do would not kill me. I am glad I did; he also talked about snakes and the ones to watch out for. He also inquired if I would be walking through the forest. I answered him honestly, saying I had no real plan, other than to just follow the Godavari River. He told me that I should not have any problems with the snakes as long as I kept out of the long grass. That was good advice. As I would be travelling alone, getting bitten by a viper, with no one around, could be fatal. Walking anywhere near grass, I needed to be loud and carry a stick. If a snake hears you coming, it will usually move out of the way.

The doctor, just like Robert, showed concern for my safety and thought I was a bit crazy doing this unplanned and unguided. He asked me if I had trained for this walk, I replied 'yes' but the truth was, I hadn't. I was fit, but training to walk 1200 kilometres over sixty days would have been impossible. Training to walk long distances takes a lot of time and that was something I didn't have. I just thought I would learn while I was walking, get stronger on the job. But the doctor did make it clear that my biggest problem would be the heat of the Indian summer. He said I would need to be hydrated at all times. I asked about the availability of water; he assured me that bottled water would be available in every village throughout India. But he didn't comment on how far one village could be to the next. He said I would need to take hydration salts with me; his advice was taken and they were packed.

Robert stopped on the journey and I bought him breakfast from a road side café. He ordered for me and I had really no idea what I ate. I suppose this was something else I would learn on the walk. Living in Mumbai, food was easy to order or make; I had the feeling walking through rural India ordering food would not be the same and nowhere near as easy.

We drove through Nashik and on to Trimbak. This was where the source of the Godavari was situated, and this was where I was to begin my adventure. I had planned to stay in an ashram (traditionally, the home of a spiritual master or teacher. People go there on retreat to seek guidance and spiritual wisdom). This ashram had opened its doors to the outside world, offering a budget bed and breakfast like scenario to people passing through the town – only not for single men like me. Here it was families only. The first mini plan that I had made was already in pieces and I had not even started the walk! Maybe being unplanned was the best way forward after all. Robert drove around to find a hotel where I could stay and after being a bit fussy about my choice, I found one. Just by chance, it was at the bottom of the small mountain I would need to climb to seek out the source of the river.

I said goodbye to Robert who, despite struggling to lift it, helped carry my rucksack into the hotel.

Then it hit me.

I was here ... I was alone ... and ready to go!

Robert, my driver

Chapter 7
Monkey Attack

The hotel I was staying in wasn't ideal, but it was in a good location. It was situated at the bottom of the Bhahmagiri Hills, the small mountain that I had to climb to see the source of the Godavari River.

Setting my mosquito net up, I decided to leave my heavy rucksack in the hotel and then asked directions to start my walk. Due to the steepness of this hill, I would have walk to the source and then retrace my footsteps back to the hotel before I set off tomorrow following the river. It was the start of my trip, but I hoped it would be the only bit of walking where I had to retrace my route.

It wasn't long before I found myself walking up steep steps. The temperature in the early afternoon heat was about 45 degrees. But I had been told I could purchase water on the way and the walk would take approximately three hours. However, I wasn't told about the monkeys.

 Walking up the mountain, I looked down and the scenery below was fantastic. It felt so good to be out of mad Mumbai and to be walking in rural India. Climbing higher, I could see a small dam that was fed by the great Godavari River and it was the first time I had seen it.

I was excited and realised that I would be spending the next two months looking at this great river. Eager to find its source and still taking photographs, I increased my pace to get to the top and see and taste the water. The climb got steeper and steeper and I knew it had been a good idea leaving my rucksack behind. I am not sure I would have been able to carry it up to the top of the mountain and down again. I then had an obvious thought … if I couldn't carry it for three hours, how was I hoping to carry it for six hours every day for next sixty days?

After about forty five minutes of walking I was stopped by some people that were descending the hill. I asked them how much further it would be before I reached the top. They advised me that it would take at least another one and a half hours.

 They also advised me to be careful of the monkeys and one man gave me his old wooden stick. He said I would need it. I thought if I had known that this was going to be such a steep walk, I would have brought my own walking sticks. But it wasn't until later that I found that the stick I had been gifted wasn't to help me walk; it was for protection against the monkeys. The man also told me hang onto my pink hat as the monkeys would look to steal it. Taking all the advice on board, I was quite worried about these monkeys before I had even set eyes on one.

I had known monkeys like to steal: hats, handbags and a variety of other items and I had even experienced it first hand, here in India, when the family visited Elephanta Island, a small island just off of Mumbai. Here, the monkeys managed to steal my son Andrew's orange juice from out of his hand when he was just walking along. However, these monkeys were just grabbing what they could, and were not aggressive, so the fact I had been advised to carry a stick did make me wonder what the monkeys here were.

It wasn't long before I came across these creatures. They were slightly bigger than their relatives on Elephanta Island, so when I walked past the first troop, I had my wooden stick in one hand and I held onto my pink hat with the other. This wasn't easy, concentrating on the monkeys, whilst trying to walk up steep steps, holding a rope to keep myself from falling back down the mountain. Was I really cut out for sixty days of walking in this heat? I told myself after the climb today, the rest of the walk will be flat, so head down and just keep going until you get to the top of the mountain.

Soon I caught up with a family: a mother, father and young daughter. They were accompanied by two teenagers. With not too much conversation, we sort of just joined each other and walked together, safety in numbers. There was a language problem, but my female pink hat caused a stir and the two teenagers were laughing at me.

They especially laughed when a monkey approached and I used my wooden stick to fend it off whilst holding my pink hat firmly to my head.

Finally, we reached the summit, where the views were spectacular. I asked someone where the source was and I was directed down a long path, past a few temples. You had to enter an outside temple, taking your shoes off, passing through the temple to find the Hindu priest sitting beside a giant well.

This was the source of the Godavari; my journey had begun. I followed the people through the temple until we reached the well and putting my stick and hat down, I sat with these people looking down into the well. The priest began to bless the people I had been walking with, giving flowers and then using a pulley system, slowly dropped a cup into the well and pulled up some water. Sacred water from the great river. I watched and really wanted to be part of this blessing. I figured if I was blessed now, at the start of my journey, this could only help me to realise my dream. Eventually the priest called me over and I was told to sit cross legged facing him, sitting about a foot away from the well. I was ready to be blessed. I had watched and followed the people who had been blessed before me. The priest indicated, with no English, to repeat after him. My Hindi was not good, even though I had learnt a bit from teaching English in the Mumbai slum school.

I had to concentrate and repeat what he was saying, which was difficult. My language skills are not the best and soon the priest had realised this.

He was trying to keep focus, but because of my terrible pronunciation, he couldn't help but smile and even laugh. I noticed that he was giving me an easier blessing to repeat compared with the people before, maybe knowing I was struggling to repeat accurately, or just because I was a foreigner. Either way, I still had to sit there for what seem like an age, repeating words with no idea what they meant. This repetitive cycle continued for over five minutes. I gave a small donation of 50 rupees and, after seeing the source, I was ready to leave. It was a magical place. I walked back through the temple; monkeys were everywhere, just sitting on the walls, staring. I didn't pay them much attention, accept to acknowledge that they were bigger and looked more aggressive than the ones I had passed earlier, at the foot of the mountain. Walking away from the well and the temple, one of the teenagers reminded me not to forget to take my wooden stick. He handed it to me and smiled. It wasn't until I left the temple that I realised what a stroke of luck it had been that he had passed me that stick.I exited along a path going towards another temple, nestled in the furthest corner at the top the mountain.

I looked at it and thought that as I had come this far, even though I only really wanted to see the source of the river, I should pay this temple a visit.

I estimated it would be a ten-minute walk and being in such an atmospheric place with wonderful scenery, I thought that I should probably see everything I could, not knowing if I would ever return.

But it was not long before I realized I was being followed along the temple path. I stopped and less than ten metres behind me was a large male monkey. I stopped and looked at it; it also stopped and stared back. Feeling braver, it started to approach me and appeared to have no attention of stopping. My saving grace was my wooden stick. I pointed it towards the monkey, showing my intentions for it to go away. I shouted at it, thinking this would perhaps scare it, but that just increased its eagerness to move closer towards me. Then it barked, louder than I had shouted and bared its teeth. It wasn't going to go away and even though my stick was held at arm's length, I knew this creature, for whatever reason, was up for a fight.

I thought back to my youth and remembered how I would never walk away from a fight, no matter how large the opponent was. As I matured, over the years, I changed my approach following Michael Jackson's words, '*I'm a lover not a fighter*', but this situation was completely different.

A Getting out of this fight, showing this creature I neither cared for nor loved him, was not going to happen.

I held my stick like a sword and was ready, at the top of this mountain, to fight this monkey. I was exposed and there were a few pathways that lead away from the temple I had planned to visit, but if I decided to out run this creature, the result could be worse than trying to scare it away. I suppose I must have looked totally pathetic: a foreign man, a small wooden stick and a pink hat shouting at a large aggressive monkey. But the truth was I was alone, with sixty days ahead of me, thinking the last thing I needed was to be bitten by this creature, stopping me completing my dream before it had begun.

So, let battle commence. I wasn't letting this creature take me down. But it wasn't long before the monkey realised that the only thing stopping him winning this fight was my stick. It showed its teeth once more and made a grab for my stick. I was tugging on it for dear life, thinking if it gets this off me, there could be teeth and claws flying around all over the place, including on my body. It was tugging so hard that I had to secure one foot against a rock and pull with all my might. I was still conscious about losing my pink hat, thinking that this was one situation that I could really do without.

But luck, (or the blessing I had received to keep me safe throughout my journey), was on my side.

The two teenagers I had been walking with just happened to be coming up the same path. The monkey's attention turned towards them, thinking perhaps they would be easier prey. I was relieved; they had laughed at me earlier for having a stick; I bet they wished they had one now. I reluctantly called to see if they needed my help. They just laughed; to them fighting off this monkey was a game. But it was a game that I didn't want to play. They indicated they didn't need my help, so I found another pathway down the mountain and away from the other temple, which after my struggle with the monkey, I decided wasn't worth the visit.

I stopped halfway down the path, still thinking that these teenagers might need my help. I turned round to watch and was just about to run back over so we could all fight this monkey away, but I stopped. The monkey was on its hind legs, attacking the trousers of one of the men. I couldn't just stand there watching so I ran closer to help. Getting nearer, the two teenagers were still laughing and enjoying themselves with monkey. But it was no laughing matter and it looked like the monkey was gaining the upper hand. I was so glad that it was not me being attacked, but soon it could be if I approached to help. The other teenager, who wasn't being attacked, had found some rocks and stones and was throwing them at the monkey to deter it, all the time laughing. Deciding my help definitely wasn't needed; I turned away and retreated back down the mountain via a long thin path.

I did encounter some more monkeys along the pathway back to the hotel, but none of them attacked me. I had escaped and, by the time I had got back to my hotel, I had been out in the heat for over four hours. I order myself a three-course meal, (curry, of course), costing less than three pounds. Then I returned to my room, settled in under my mosquito net and set the alarm for 4.00am. I tried to get to sleep as quickly as possible. The real walking would be starting tomorrow.

Monkeys! Beware!

Chapter 8
Proper Walking

It was my first day of proper walking and I knew it was going to be hard. Firstly, I over slept. I had wanted to start walking at 4.30am, but with all of yesterday's excitement, I didn't wake up until 7.00am. I had planned to walk for six hours non-stop, but including stops, I figured I would be walking for over eight hours.

I left the hotel and starting walking in the direction of the river. On this occasion, the river was nearly in sight and ran parallel with the road. I walked a few kilometres along the actual banks of the Godavari, but soon realised if I wanted to cover any distance quickly, it would be easier to follow the road. But this had its problems too. With my rucksack securely strapped to my back and walking stick in both hands,

I was prepared. But it wasn't long before I faced for the first time what would become a consistent daily problem - DOGS.

I suppose the dogs were just doing their jobs and protecting their territory. But that didn't make it any easier for me walking.

I was only on my second day and after being attacked by a monkey yesterday, to now be faced with a dog attack was something that was really stressing me out.

From a dog's point of view, I must have appeared really strange and they were just letting me know that they thought I was strange and that I was not welcome. The combination of my pink hat, heavy lump strapped to my back, white skin and two blue metal walking poles hitting the ground was not making me at all popular when I passed any dogs.

Some dogs would run away, some would just sit and watch. But most would bark, some would show their teeth and team up ready to attack. On my first day of proper walking, I experienced every possible way these dogs could treat me and I quickly realised that I had to be very careful when I heard (or saw) a dog. I would use my sticks to deter them, but just like the monkey situation, this often made the situation worse. I knew if I was going to continue to walk all the way across India, I would need to find a better way of being accepted by 'man's best friend.'

After two hours of walking, it was time for my first water stop. A litre of water cost eight pence and was consumed without the sides of my throat. I ate something that looked like a samosa. I wasn't exactly sure what it was, but it tasted alright and I was soon walking again. I had only covered only 4.5 kilometres in two hours. I had planned to walk twenty nine kilometres a day, so at this pace, it would take me over twelve hours to reach my next stop.

I quickly acknowledged that something had to change. I knew I would learn on the road what I needed to do to complete this walk, but I didn't think that this would have happened so early on in the walk.

Even after the first two hours, my shoulders were hurting a great deal. I knew they would get stronger as I walked every day, but the pain they were giving me already was a clear indication that something had to change. Having planned to walk twenty five to thirty kilometres every day for forty five to sixty days, there was no way I would achieve that at this pace, with this heavy rucksack, in this heat.

My first day's journey was from the source of the river, Trimbak, to a large town called Nashik. It was a lonely first day. I listened to some Neil Diamond to take my mind off the pain I was feeling. I stopped any time I could to drink water and change my socks. Blisters were forming and my sweaty, drenched socks were the start of this problem. Following every two hours of walking, I needed to stop, dry my feet and put on clean, fresh socks. The nightmare continued and I soon realised, what with the pain and pressure of trying to increase my pace, I had lost my sunglasses.

But I had taken a spare pair, (just in case) and with my large, pink brimmed hat, I quickly put my first disaster behind me. Later on, after many stops, my rucksack had acquired a huge split due to the weight. It really wasn't a good first day of proper walking.

Walking continued and several people on motorbikes stopped by the side of the road, offering me a lift. It was hard work explaining to them that I was walking across India and they simply couldn't understand why I didn't want to take them up on their kind offer of a ride the back of their bikes.

Richard Smith, my friend in England, phoned me. Knowing this was my first day, I needed all the encouragement I could get. We spoke as I continued to walk along the side of the road, where I got my first of many sightings of a dead animal; this one being a water buffalo and, judging by the lack of skin and the fact that the carcass was pressed almost flat into the ground, it had been there for quite some time. I had never really thought about dead animals left by the side of the road before. I suppose it is something that you don't often see, maybe the odd fox or pigeon back in the UK. But over the course of this trip I saw many.

Richard spoke and simply asked how I was and if I had really bitten off more than I could chew. As we were speaking, yet another biker stopped.

'Sir, please jump on. I will give you a lift,' he told me.

'Thank you, but I am walking to raise money for children that live in a Mumbai slum, so I need to walk whenever I can. Thank you, but I will continue to walk'.

'Sir, it is hot and I am going your way, please let me help you,' he continued.

'No, sir. I need to walk whenever I can, but thank you for stopping and asking'.

'Sir, why are you walking? India has a perfectly good transport system that runs all over India, including Maharashtra.'

At this point Richard, who was on the phone listening, just started to laugh. He, like me, knew that the people could just not understand why some white man wearing a pink hat, would choose to be walking along the road in 50 degrees heat.

After refusing several more motor bike rides, I came within the city of Nashik. I was really struggling; I had been walking for nearly eleven hours and it was getting dark. I had planned to stay at a small guest house within the city; now I just needed to find it. After getting lost a few times and asking many taxi drivers where I could locate this guest house, I finally found it. It looked more like a shop than somewhere I could sleep. Approaching the door, I was told that the man who owned the hotel was not there, so shedding the large burden from my back, I collapsed into a chair.

After sitting for what seem like an hour, the owner of the hotel arrived. Asif Monde was a lovely man and soon became my first friend.

Asif took pride in showing me around the guest house. The front part was a dairy, where a long queue of people were waiting to collect their daily milk, served from large churns and poured into plastic bags.

I had been walking all day through rural India and now I had very much found myself back in a large busy town. Wherever I looked, someone was buying or selling something. Welcome to Nashik.

Asif was concerned that his guest house would not be up to my western standards and as he showed me around, he kept repeating that this was an Indian guest house. This was to soften the shock when he showed me the rooms I had to choose from to sleep in that night. But after walking for so long, whatever the room was like, as long as it was safe, I didn't have the energy to turn it down and start looking for somewhere else to sleep. I decided on a room and was introduced to the Indian toilet - a hole in the floor. I had a look and having used one on previous travels, I convinced myself that I shouldn't have too many problems. The last time I had used such a toilet was a long time ago, when I was a younger man and a lot more flexible than I was now.

 I did wonder how I was physically going to be able to use it later, especially considering every part of my body was aching from all the walking.

I asked Asif if he could help with my split rucksack and he said knew someone that could fix this later. He asked for an hour's grace and then suggested I meet him in the dairy. So, I did. I sat waiting, watching him sell the milk, moving the large churns in and out of the shop that was connected to the guest house. Then he was ready, but he hadn't said anything about how I was going to get to the person who would fix my rucksack. Asif disappeared then reappeared, sitting on a motor bike, indicating for me to jump on. I wasn't going to refuse, even though I was a bit scared.

The traffic in Nashik was crazy and just like Mumbai, appeared to have no real rules. After less than five minutes on the back of his bike, I was taken over to a small man, sitting next to a sewing machine on the side of a road. Asif took the rucksack; the man with the machine stopped all his other jobs and sewed the tear that had developed after only one day's walking. I paid him about eight pence for his trouble and then it was back on the bike and back to the hotel. Asif stopped again and, this time, getting off the bike, I nearly tipped us both off; travelling by bike was something that I had not done too much of.

He pointed me in the right direction to buy bananas and milk and told me the best place to eat later. Then he returned me to the guest house. What service and what a great man.I returned to my room, and decide to get all my stuff ready for my next day's walking. It was then I realised that not only had I lost my sunglasses during my first proper walk, but I had also lost my sleep sheets. All in all, it had not been a good first day. My feet were killing me and my shoulders were numb. I looked at my newly stitched rucksack, leaning against the wall under the only window in the room. I knew the weight I was carrying had to be reduced. Losing my sleep sheets that had been fastened to the outside of my rucksack hadn't lightened the load that much. I decided to empty the rucksack and be tough and get rid of more stuff that I didn't think I would need. This was not easy it was Day 2 of my walk, with no real plan ahead of me other than to get to the other side of this country. Knowing what to leave behind was an almost impossible task, I was also very tired and other than breakfast and the odd banana, I hadn't eaten all day. There I was, with all that I owned, sitting on my single, hard, wooden hotel bed. All my possessions there, looking at me saying, 'please don't throw me away, you might need me later'. I looked at the six pairs of woollen socks and, after the heat of my first day's walking, they could be the first to be left behind. Then batteries for my portable sat nav; I figured if my phone had worked giving me directions today, then it would probably work for the rest of the trip.

Moisturiser, spare shampoo and soap - all were given up. I looked and I couldn't really risk leaving anything else behind.Running my eyes over the sacrificed items, sitting there in the corner of the room, I felt good that I had managed to lighten my load; any little weight loss would make this journey easier for me to achieve. I closed the hotel door, only to be met by a total power cut. The torch on my phone saved me and I managed to get to the entrance of the guest house, where the dairy was still in full working order; people were still buying milk in the darkness. I saw Asif and explained that I would be leaving some things in the corner of the room so not to contact me after I had left tomorrow, thinking I had forgotten something.   I told him if he could find any use for it, he could have it. I got a strange flash in my mind of him walking around the guest house and dairy in the darkness, wearing my woolly socks.The power was still off and I asked what time it would be coming back on. I was just weighing up if I could be bothered to venture out of the guest house to find somewhere to eat or not. I looked along the street and the whole town seemed to be in darkness. This made the idea of finding a restaurant even harder to face. I was really hungry earlier but now, I almost felt too tired to eat. My body was still in shock with what I had put it through this first day of proper walking. Maybe just a few more bananas and then to bed. I sat, still watching the dairy in full operation, not really having the energy to climb the stairs to get to bed. My feet were starting to show the first signs of blistering and I really noticed it when

I had to walk either up or down stairs. So, there I sat, waiting to recharge and chatting with Asif, who said that in the morning at 4.30am, he would be around to point me in the right direction for my walk to start to tomorrow. I was about to call it a night when, just by chance, my second friend of the day appeared. This man started talking to me about how good India had been during Queen Victoria's reign. Before I knew it, I was on the back of his bike, off exploring. I was really tired but determined to see as much as I could, so I put the tiredness out of my mind. It turned out that Kausar owned vineyards and hotels in the area. I tried to resist, but he wanted to take me to dinner at one of the hotels he owned. Within an hour, I had been on two motor bikes. I am walking India in the morning and seeing how many vehicles I can get on at night. We walked into his restaurant, the food was ordered and his friend joined us. What a lovely man. He reminded me of Al Pacino. We ate chicken kebabs; this meal turned out to be the first and last time I was to eat meat on my whole adventure. I wasn't worried about the chicken and felt at ease with my new friend who was being so kind, showing me around and feeding me. But when the food came out covered in a white sauce, I was nearly sick eating it (I don't eat sauces of any kind). But he was showing me his country and being kind, so I just continued to eat it. This reminded me of a scene in *All Creatures Great and Small*, where one of the vets was forced to eat tripe and ate it so as not to offend. I held it down and was so pleased to just meet someone that would go out of their way to help and feedd me. Another great person and, here I was, on my second day and already I had met two people that had helped me. I was blown away by their help and kindness and was amazed by the people of this great country.

True to his word, after the dinner, we just walked out of the restaurant. It seemed funny having no bill to worry about. Then, back on the bike and back to my hotel.
Al Pacino said we'd only be an hour and we were. I thanked him, went into the hotel and straight to bed.

Al Pacino and his friend

Chapter 9
Prekash's Farm

After such an eventful day yesterday, I surprised myself being up and ready to walk at 4.30am. Saying goodbye to Asif at the reception, he pointed me the right direction and it wasn't long before I was walking along the road again in the dark.

I had decided to wear my trainers today, because blisters were starting to form. I thought by changing my footwear it would give my feet a different experience and maybe even stop the development of the blisters caused by my walking boots. It was so much better starting in the morning and after walking with a torch for a bit, it was a good feeling watching the sun coming up. The best thing was walking for two hours non-stop and not feeling the direct blistering heat of the sun. I had planned a twenty six kilometres walk ahead of me and I estimated it would take me around six hours of solid walking. I stopped after two hours and I am glad that I did. Walking along the side of a road, I came across a hut-like café selling food and water.

It was a popular place and, like most of these places, was situated at the roads' intersection. I bought some water, sat down and took care of my feet. I had to change my socks and plasters, (which were soaking wet with sweat), using the essentials of talcum powder and Vaseline.

People were just staring at me; they were not being rude. They had just never seen a white person here, especially a white person walking and fixing their feet. I wasn't shocked or surprised that a crowd of thirty people formed, just standing, watching me. They asked me in broken English and Hindi what I was doing. It was here that I was lucky to meet yet another friend that, without this chance meeting, who knows what could have happened to me. His name was Prekash, and was I glad I had met him.

He asked me where I was going and why, so I told him. He was the first person who really understood my quest and the reasons for it. He looked at Google maps and when I told him where I was going, he told me it was the wrong route. I tried to explain my plan, but he told me that I could not go direct and I could not follow the river all the way due to the lack of accommodation. He took my number and said he would find somewhere for me to stay. I thanked him and went on my way. I couldn't hang around; walking past midday is dangerous, with the temperatures.

I passed my first school; children came out to see me. They were fascinated by me and wanted to practise their English. I did think about going in, but it was a secondary school, and time was moving on. I needed to keep walking and get out of the heat as quickly as possible.

After more than three hours walking, I reached a junction; not too far to the hotel now. My feet were killing me; the blisters had certainly started. Then Prakash phoned.

'John, stay where you are; you can stay on my sister's farm,' he insisted.

I stopped at another drinking hut and did as he asked. But just as I started drinking my sixth litre of water, a man arrived on a motorbike and told me to jump on. Another motor bike? That was three different bikes I had been on in the last two days and I thought I was meant to be walking across India. This man told me his name was Tushar. He drove me miles off the main road and all sorts of thoughts ran through my mind. Here I was, jumping on the back of a complete stranger's bike, not knowing where I was going and with whom I would be spending the night.

This was real rural India and I was enjoying the rest. But could this not be just a little bit dangerous? Why would someone go so much out of their way to help me? Was this a plan to get me off the road and then mug me? However, I didn't sense anything other than good will. In my time, I have done a lot of travelling and you get a feeling in your stomach if something isn't right, but sitting on the back of this stranger's bike didn't feel in the least bit wrong. Tushar was Prekash's brother-in-law.

He tried to talk to me in broken English and soon I knew I was in safe hands. He asked me if I was a friend of Prekash and I said yes. He explained that Prekash had asked him to collect me from the roadside and take me back to their farm. I think he was asking how long I had known Prekash, I thought about answering this question honestly and explaining that I had only just met him in roadside hut four hours earlier, but thought that did not sound particularly good. I just said Prekash is a good friend of mine and what wonderful man he is. Tushar agreed and after only meeting Prekash four hours ago, he was a friend and so was this man whose bike I was sitting on. It was unbelievable to think that from the moment I started walking, people were so ready to help me, but more than help: to feed me, shelter me, guide me and give advice so I could continue on my journey. Friendships in this country seem easy to strike up.

'If you do someone a favour, it is the best way to make a friend,' Benjamin Franklin stated. So true. These people were helping me and therefore they considered themselves to be my friends and they were.Back in the UK, I looked at friendship in a totally different way. People you have known all your life and the people you have grown up with and shared good times with are your friends. But it is very rare that you meet good friends as you age and go through life.

You might meet someone, enjoy their company and have good times, but after you move on, how many do you stay in touch with?

How many do you really make an effort with and after the years go by, how many do you still speak to?

It didn't feel like that here in India; people you meet want to stay in touch and at this moment in time, so do I. Tashur pulled into an enormous drive way, past an old tractor and a massive cow in the yard, eating some freshly picked vegetation.

The farm was huge with all sorts of crops – grain, sugar cane, you name it. I got off the bike and met all Tashur's family: his wife, his two children and both his parents. They were a bit shocked, but after a while they realized I was just an ordinary, mad English man, lost and on a mission.

Tushar was the only one that could speak any English, but that didn't matter. I was made so welcome. First, a shower, then I was shown to my room. My luck had changed; it didn't take long for these people to accept me. But my feet were absolutely killing me.

Then something amazing happened. Tushar's mother took over. She cut me some fresh aloe vera from the farm and got me water. I sat on the step just looking at my sore feet. I was limping and finding it difficult to put any weight on either foot. I knew I had to move on tomorrow but the reality of that seemed to be more and more impossible.

I took the natural aloe vera that Tashur's mother had gave me, mixing it with my antiseptic cream, thinking that nature, combined with the magic of Savlon, (the best cream I have ever used), could only double the chances of producing a miracle and make it possible for me to continue walking the next day.

The mother was concerned looking at my blisters, shaking her head, she said something in Hindi, probably something like, 'he must be mad and there is no way he will be able to walk the whole way across India'.

She was so concerned that she got a bucket of water, filled it with salt and told me to soak my feet in. This was obviously meant to happen before I had put the cream and aloe vera on my poor feet. But she was so concerned, she wanted to massage them. I had only just met this lady, who was, I would say, in her late sixties at least and she was prepared to let me stay the night, feed me and now massage my feet. I had to stop her, not because I didn't want her to help me, but her kindness was just too much for me to take in. Words can't explain an act of kindness and concern of that nature and magnitude. I was wondering if I would ever experience anything else like that again? Her name was Shantabaee Tarle.

I played with Tushar's children and it wasn't long before they both had accepted me and we were playing hide and seek, even though my feet were hurting so much I could never venture far enough to find them.

Then they dressed up wearing all sorts of fancy vivid coloured hats. I had been let into their house and within two hours, with no common language amongst us, I was accepted as part of their family. It didn't feel false like they had to let me stay; it was totally genuine and it was like I had known these people for years.

Deepali, Tahsur's wife, made me lunch and served it while I just sat there, resting my feet. Tushar returned and we spoke broken English and Hindi to try and understand each other. I was so grateful for these complete strangers helping me. It doesn't matter how you communicate, if both parties want to, you can get by. What wonderful people. I was then sitting, writing this blog (which is all I do any spare moment that I have got), when all of a sudden everyone, including the two young children, started to panic and run around. The rain was coming. I went outside and saw the whole family trying to move the grain that was drying outside under cover. I went to help, but Tushar told me to sit down. No way was I going to sit down and watch. For the next fifteen minutes, we all worked like slaves to get the grain into big sacks and under cover. Three generations of the family, along with myself, working as fast as we could. Hand, buckets, large plastic bins, anything was used to collect the grain from the ground and move it out of the rain. They couldn't believe I was helping, but I didn't see it as strange, even though I was hobbling due to my blisters, I enjoyed it.

We had just finished getting all of it into the dry when the heavens opened up. These farmers knew how to read the clouds. We all just sat there, watching the rain fall. I could safely say this was the best and most relaxed place in the whole of India I had visited so far; I felt at completely at peace. I was in the country away from any busy city and with a family whose company I was really enjoying.

Later we picked some sugar cane, which was then squeezed into a drink; *green sugar drink* as they called it. After that, a tour of the farm while dinner was being prepared. We just sat on the ground in a field, appreciating the clean, open space of the farm, Tushar sat next to me in the grass field that had been left to pasture, his children ran free; I watched them and they were happy. Young men from other local farms had heard that there was a stranger in their neighbourhood and they had come to meet me. Not much English was spoken, but as many as ten young men shook my hand and just took a seat on the ground; we all watched the day fall into dusk. The sun was setting and the evening meal was being prepared. I felt so comfortable I could easily have stayed with this family for weeks, just helping them work on their farm.

Evening arrived.

Deepali was offended because I had done my own washing earlier. She couldn't believe that I had washed my clothes in a bucket in the bathroom, and was even more shocked when I attempted to hang them on the line. It was very much a women's job to carry out work that was connected to the house. I tried to explain that I was grateful for her help, but I could hang my own washing out. She looked at me, very upset, so I said 'thank you', and let her take over. There was definitely no way she was going to let me help with anything to do the preparation of the food.

So, when the sun went down and us boys had had enough of playing and relaxing, it was time to eat. Prekash had turned up with his daughter and we were fed first in the lounge, while the women and children ate later (and separately), in the kitchen. The food was spicy and, of course, vegetarian; it was lovely. But I just seemed to have a problem eating it. I think my body was in shock and not prepared to take on any excess food that would hinder my walking. I tried to explain to Deepali that her cooking was lovely, I was just not that hungry, but again she just gave me the same disappointing look she had given me earlier when I wanted to do my own washing. After dinner, we spoke in Hindi and broken English, but the communication was easier now that Prekash had arrived. Then it was time to go to bed.

Tushar fixed my mosquito net and it was decided that I would
meet Prekash in the morning, as he was going to come back for
me at 4.30 am to give me a lift back to civilisation and onto the
main road.

I pumped up my inflatable mattress, as the bed was so hard,
and the lights when out. My feet were still hurting and I knew
that to reach my goal, to walk over twenty five kilometres, I
would need to get up early in the morning. Preparing my feet
before I started to walk, with plasters, talcum powder and
Vaseline would take over forty five minutes, so the quicker I
could go to sleep, the quicker I could move on. I did think
about asking to stay at this farm for another day, because it
was so peaceful, but my mission just told me to keep on
moving.

I had been lying down for no more than ten minutes when
there was a knock on my door. It was Prekash.

'To save me returning in the morning, would it be ok if I was to
sleep here with you tonight?' he asked.

At first, I thought that this was a strange request and all sorts
of negative thoughts darted through my head. A strange house
in the middle of nowhere with another man that I had only
just met earlier sleeping in the same room as me.

'Of course, do you want the bed? I will sleep on the floor' I
replied.

But to Prekash, I was the guest in his sister's house, so he took the floor. The lights when out and then he started to speak. What a great person, I was thinking. He had gone out of his way to look after me and now I was speaking to him and sharing a room in the pitch darkness.

He spoke about the countryside - a long story how he was lying in bed one night sleeping with the whole of his family, when a large viper had landed on his head. He said he was lucky, but he woke his family and moved them into another room. Then he re-entered the room, armed with a hammer, killed the snake, threw it out of the back door, recollected his family and then went back to sleep.

I was lying in this dark room, in the middle of the countryside, with all sorts of scary thoughts going through my mind. Prekash continued to talk. He was a wise man, and I was listening. After ten more minutes of conversation and just before I was about to drift off to sleep, Prakash said:

'John. Just a warning. If you need the toilet in the night, don't go outside'.

'Why?'

'Because there are leopards.'

'Really?'

On Day 1 Robert, my driver, had warned me about them, but I hadn't really thought much more about it.

Then Prakash said 'if I was in your country you would expect me to listen to you, wouldn't you?'

'Yes.'

'Well, my friend, you are in my country, so please take my advice.'

'Of course.'

'Oh, and that tent. Don't use it.'

I replied 'it's already gone', and that was the moment my load got lighter and worries of being eaten alive vanished. I decided to leave it there so the young children could play with it. So, at 4.30 in the morning, the whole family was up and I was setting the tent upin the kitchen. Another really strange situation.

The room I had slept in was huge and it wasn't until the morning that I noticed most of the family had slept together in the lounge. I didn't know if that was to accommodate me being there, or if they slept like that every night. Prekash gave me a lift on his bike to the main road, and I said 'goodbye' and started another long day of walking. I thought about how if I hadn't meet Prekash I would never had met his wonderful family or had the chance to stay on a farm.

 But more importantly, I would still be carrying the tent, and I had had every intention of using it, so thank god I was advised not to. But with no tent, it would mean that I had to find proper accommodation every night, which could to be a real challenge. But no tent meant less chance of meeting a leopard and being eaten!

Thank you Prekash, I shall never forget your help and sound advice.

Prakesh, a friend is someone you need

Neil Diamond once sung a song with the line: '*A friend is someone you need*' and I certainly needed to meet him.

Chapter 10
Feet Failure

After saying goodbye to Prekash, the road was all that was in front of me. I felt strong and the rucksack was so much more bearable without the tent. But my feet with their four blisters, two on each foot, were really sore. Two were on each heel and the remaining two were under my toes in the middle of my foot. The left foot under the toes was the worse and it was starting to change colour and it looked yellow. I would have to keep a close eye on that.

Prekash phoned as I was walking and asked if I was ok. I said I was, but that couldn't have been further from the truth. I was in a lot of pain, and I just needed to keep on walking to my next stop; another large town called Niphal. I made several stops whilst I was walking and I was getting a bit concerned that I was not eating much at all and, in fact, I didn't even feel like eating. Maybe it was the heat and the pain I was in, but since starting I had had to force myself to eat. Eventually after walking another full day and coving twenty kilometres,

I had reached the outskirts of the town and found a guest house.

I was waiting around trying firstly, to find a bed for the day and then assess my feet situation, when I got a bad feeling, that somehow, this didn't feel safe.

There seemed to be no one around and all of a sudden, lots of teenage boys turned up on their bikes, telling me to wait while they found the owner of the guest house. The room I was shown was massive, with two rooms, a separate bathroom and a bedroom. It really looked too much for just me to stay, but I was just ready to stay anywhere considering the blisters of my feet were killing me. However, after several teenagers telling me to wait in the bedroom, I decide that it just didn't feel right. With my experience of travelling, whenever you get a small feeling that something isn't right, it is important to heed those feelings. So, I dragged myself out of the guest house and hit the road. I bought a pineapple for that was the only thing that I felt I could eat.

Finally, two kilometres later, I reached another hotel that I decided I would stay in. I had walked 15 kilometres and it had taken me all morning.

I knew I would have to increase the distance walked if I wanted to get across this massive country. Before I tried to check in, I sat at a little shack-come restaurant at the side of the road, (there are lots of them everywhere). I ordered my usual litre of water, cold water or thanda paanee (ठंडा पानी) as they say around here.

A man entered the restaurant, saw me and came over to speak English. We talked in broken English and then it was time for me to get out my golden ticket. This is an English sentence, translated into Hindi, on a laminated piece of paper that was written by one of the teachers in the slum school. The sentence explains my mission. She said it would help and it certainly had done so far.

People can't really understand why I am walking. People stop on the road and offer me lift. I refuse. One man asked 'where is your vehicle? If you come from England, surely you can afford a bike?'

Anyway, the golden ticket was passed around the restaurant. This man then bought me lunch. His name was Rushikesh. Later, the owner of the restaurant gave me tea and a cream horn, which I struggled to eat but there was no way I was going to leave it uneaten. Generosity like this was their way of giving to the charities I am supporting. It was amazing how wonderful these people were. It made me cry and also made me realise that the majority of people in this world are good. I am not a religious person, but there is a lot to be said for faith - whether we believe or don't believe in something. There are things that our minds cannot understand and there are things that we simply must be grateful for; this trip was showing me that.

So, after people had helped me, I would shake their hand, I found myself putting my hands together in a praying gesture, just as the Hindi people do (*namaste*). I don't why I started to do this but somehow it helped to thank them in a more believable way.

So, this is where my story began and I will never forget this hotel. After struggling to make it to the room, crying in pain, I collapsed on the bed, realising I needed to get to the bathroom to get ready for the operation I had in mind. Here I discovered swarms of mosquitos, so before I could operate on my feet, I was flapping around the bathroom trying to kill as many mosquitos as possible. I managed to get quite a few, each one bursting, full of blood. It might seem a minor problem compared to my feet; however, I knew that if I saw that many mosquitos full of someone else's blood, I had to try to kill as many as I could.

After all the advice not to burst my blisters, I decided it was the only way release the liquid built up in my left foot. Job done, puss released, I lay on the bed, taking deep breaths. I had 900 kilometres still to walk and I was only on day 4 of my trip and, looking at the ceiling, I shed a tear. My dreams of finishing this trip were vanishing. I had been beaten at the first hurdle and my feet simply could not carry on. It was a sad moment. I considered myself a failure.

====

I woke up at my usual time of 4.00am and no matter how bad a situation is, sleeping on it can sometimes make a world of difference. The first thing I did was to assess the feet situation. They were hurting so much they had even disturbed my sleep in the night. My feet were shot; the obvious truth was that I could not continue. The blister that had been burst last night would not allow me to walk the planned twenty five kilometres today; this would only make this situation worse. Failure was the only thought that kept echoing around my mind and I don't do failure easily.

What was I going to do? Call the whole trip off after only four days of walking? I would be a laughing stock and, more importantly, I would have let my charities down and those people that were supporting me. I had flashes of all the poor children's faces that I teach in the slum. I would be letting them all down. But the biggest person I was letting down was myself.

There had to be a way I could continue this trip and save some dignity.

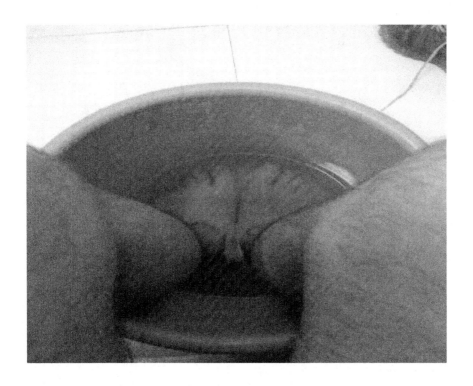

A daily salt water soak was becoming the norm

Who Wants To Be A Millionaire?

My wife's advice was to just get across India any way you can. She told me straight: 'you are no Bear Grylls, you are just a mad school teacher on a mission'. I had to remember this advice several times during the trip; think before you leap.

I wasn't the sort of person that would just sit in the hotel and wait for the blisters to mend. I estimated that it would be at least two days before I could continue walking any distance. I decided that while I was here, I would do some sightseeing; see some things that were near to where I had stopped. I decided that if I travelled on a bus to places of interest, I would not be promoting my journey in any way. So, whilst I was out of action, a mini plan was formed.

To ease the boredom, I decided to jump on a bus, but this was not as easy as I had anticipated. The buses were all so crowded and fighting just to get on one, especially with a large rucksack, was a feat in itself. It was only after clambering on the first bus that I realised how much better it was to walk. It was also here that I split my trousers. The freedom of the open space was a sharp reminder that I needed to get back to walking as soon as possible.

It also highlighted one of the reasons that I had decided to go ahead with this trip - to make people aware of the wonders of the natural freedom of walking.

On the bus, I pin-pointed a destination of a nearby small town where I thought I could firstly, rest up and secondly, see some of the many temples I had not had time to explore whilst walking. After many lost in translation conversations, I found myself heading to a place called Shrirampur. Shrirampur is the third biggest city in Ahmednagar district, situated in western Maharashtra. Getting there was more difficult than I anticipated; in fact, I had to get several buses because there was no direct route. When I arrived, I felt more tired than I did after a day's walking, but I easily found a hotel near the bus station and after finding something quick to eat, I was soon lying on the bed, resting my blisters.

Not being able to walk and having some time on my hands, I ventured out to do some sight-seeing. I decided to take a closer look at my boots, thinking these could be the reason for the problems that have caused the blisters.

After close examination, I found that I had no innersoles in the boots and there was a harsh needle mark joining the boots together that ran straight down the middle of the sole. Could this be the reason I was getting blisters under my toes? I decided that whilst being in a town I would find a shoe shop where I could buy some innersoles; I also took the opportunity to top up on mosquito spray, more plaster tape and shampoo.

After walking the streets and getting all my shopping, I hobbled out of Shririampur and walked through a small community, with water buffaloes moseying around and, sometimes in, the people's houses. The people were friendly and soon I had a crowd following me.

As I walked around, I kept bumping into a man with a broken arm. I asked him how he had broken it and he explained that he had fallen off his bike. He further went onto explain in broken English that, because he has broken his arm, he couldn't work as fast as he needed to and that his family were struggling to find enough money to eat. A real reminder that in rural India people are living so close to the poverty line that one serious injury to any member of the family who brings money home can simply mean the difference between eating and not eating. Even though this man was down on his luck, I was amazed how friendly he was and he took great pleasure showing me around his house.

His house was a shack of corrugated metal and blue plastic sheeting. The whole of his house, including a wife and three children, were all confined in one room. This would not have been an unusual situation in any place in India, but what shocked me was the amount of rubbish that these people had with them, within this room. There was hardly any space for anyone to sleep, or just to be.

Plastic bottles, cardboard, empty food tins, anything that you could imagine that could be traded for cash, was crammed, floor to ceiling, against the four tin walls. I didn't stay too long, as I felt completely useless. The man was proud of what he had, but just worried that because of his injury, he was not pulling his weight. It would be a perfect world if I could physically help every person that I met, but I knew I couldn't. I shook the man's hand, the one that was not broken, and left with a smile.

Leaving the man's house, I was soon swamped by local men. I had gone from seeing a man's misfortunes to entering the life of the famous, just because I was a rare sight in these parts. It was selfie time and I am not joking when I say that I must have had forty selfies in a half an hour. It seems that only the young men have mobile phones that are capable of taking selfies and phones were passed around through the crowd. With all this attention, I took the opportunity to ask where the local school was. There were at least ten young men that were happy to show me the way.

I walked down several alleys and found my first school. I was invited in and was shocked by how small the classroom was. The children were still using slate boards; no pens, no paper, no desks, and no chairs. I sat with the children for a bit and tried to help them with their work. Only maths seemed the way forward. No one spoke any English.

There were about fifteen children and two old ladies and, after some broken English, I discovered that one was the teacher; the other was just a helper. I don't know what I expected when I saw my first school, but in some ways, it seemed even poorer that the slum school I was teaching in back in Mumbai. Even though it was a rural school, it somehow seemed to look and feel like it was in a large city. It must have been the walk down the small narrow streets that gave me the impression that I was in a town or city. It almost felt like I had taken a time machine back to the past and, at any moment, Charles Dickens, or one of his book characters, would appear. After spending less than an hour within the crowded classroom, I left the school. Turning a few corners in the cobbled stoned alley ways, I came face to face with some water buffalos; a true wake-up call that I was indeed in rural India.   I walked back to the hotel for something to eat. This is when I met Satis.

I walked into the restaurant and looked around. Everyone stopped and looked up. A white person here was rarer than pure gold. That line from Sting's *'English Man in New York'* song came to mind: *'I'm an alien, I'm a legal alien'*. But this certainly wasn't New York! Then a man said in English 'please sit here'. Wow, someone that could speak English. I joined him and he told me his name is Satis.

Satis, like lots of Indian men, wore a dark black moustache and this was the first thing I noticed about him. Someone told me that the length or thickness of an Indian man's moustache is a sign of their masculinity.

I was also told that the size of moustache can determine a man's ranking within the police force. I am not sure if this was true, but Satis' moustache helped outline his smile and that was one of his main features. Satis was a large man and, I guess that spending a lot of time on his own (which I later found out he did), had made him more fond of his food. Eating out was something I thought Satis enjoyed and did a lot of.

Straightaway, Satis started talking in broken English and once he began, there was no stopping him. First, he named all the counties in England: Derbyshire, Lancashire, Somerset etc...
Then he started naming all the English cricket players from years past: Vaughan, Gough, Botham etc. I just looked at him and asked what he was eating and ordered the same. He then said 'could you offer me a soft drink?'

I said 'it doesn't work like that', but I bought him a Sprite anyway.

He then asked me so many questions about England – I can't remember them all – but the strangest was 'what brands of ice cream do you get in England?'
We exchanged numbers and I thought 'what an unusual man'. I said goodbye and hit the hotel for sleep. Later, Satis phoned me. I explained I needed to sleep as I was walking tomorrow.

The next morning, on further examination, I decided the blisters were still so bad that I needed to rest up for another day. Luckily the blister I was particularly worried about had not become infected, but it still wasn't up to walking. Paying for another night's accommodation, I was bored and a bit down. Were these blisters going to get any better and allow me to carry on my mission?

In the evening, Satis phoned again and was over-joyed that I was still in his town. I met him in the evening and the same list of names and question were fired at me. After another meal and me buying him more Sprite, he asked if I would like to jump on his bike and see his church and some other churches in the area. Not really, I thought, but how could I say no? I wanted an early night, but yet again found myself on the back of a motor bike.

First, we visited a Catholic Church. Here I met the priest who blessed me and my journey. We then went on to Satis' church and were surrounded, yet again, by people who wanted to see a white man. He was persistent and kept riding around town, pointing out all the churches. He thought that with me being an English man, we had something in common and that was churches. He was a good man.

We returned to the hotel and I bought him a snack and a cup of chai this time. He started the questions and lists again. I thought this was really strange.

He then told me his secret: he had been on India's version of
Who Wants to be a Millionaire and he'd won a crore! [A crore
is ten million rupees (or one hundred lacs)].

That's around £107,700.00 to us. Was he really telling me the
truth, or had he just watched '*Slum Dog Millionaire*'? He
continued with his story and told me the money was in the
bank and he was going to use it to travel to England. The
penny suddenly dropped for me; that's why he knew so many
lists of names, and never stopped asking general knowledge
questions.

We parted; back to walking tomorrow. As I returned to my
hotel, I asked myself why, if Satis had just won that amount of
money on *Who Wants to be a Millionaire*, was I the one
buying all the Sprites?

Satis and his motorbike.

Chapter 12
Donkey Days

Day 6 and, after resting up for the last few days, the brain started to play tricks on me. I knew that I would have a lot of thinking time ahead of me, but I expected all the thinking would be taking place whilst I was walking, but that had not been the case. With my feet being out of action, I have had plenty of time to think, most of the time just lying on a hotel bed resting my feet. I was certainly at a low and I hadn't even really started the arduous journey ahead of me.

The true facts of this mission were not going away. I had set out on this trip, deliberately not having a plan except to follow the Godavari River from its source to its end. But after the second day, I followed the river when I could but, due to its remoteness, that was not really feasible. I had nowhere to stay and the tent was a distant memory and no longer an option, with the risk of being eaten by wild leopards. It was impossible to follow the river all the way and I had a larger problem to face up to and that was, where was I going to sleep every night? I had realised with the scorching heat, to walk any more than twenty to twenty five kilometres a day would be complete madness, but if I increased the distance walked every day in order to find somewhere to sleep, I think I would be in danger of not finishing the trip at all.

I would be walking through some of the remotest areas of rural India and the problem I had to face was that there was no accommodation between small settlements. Some small towns and villages were as much as fifty to eighty kilometres apart, so there was no way I could make it from one accommodation place to the next. I acknowledged this problem as I studied the map; my route took me into less populated countryside with no accommodation. I had planned to walk all the way and now I knew that would not be possible. I had failed.

How could I continue? I had two options; neither of which I particularly liked, but if I was going to keep going, I had to take one or the other.

Option 1: This would be to set out walking and walk my twenty to twenty five kilometres a day, stop and rely on someone being there to look after me and let me sleep in their house or drive me to the next point of available accommodation.

Option 2: To catch a bus (or a lift) first thing in the morning to get myself within an achievable walking distance of around twenty to twenty five kilometres to the next village and a place to sleep.

These were my only choices available that would allow me to continue this journey across this vast country. It was a sick feeling, knowing that to achieve my goal, I would not be physically capable of walking all the way. The same words kept echoing around my mind 'I had failed.'

I had to keep telling myself that there was nothing I could do. I had attempted this unplanned and unsupported and what I had in front of me now was a situation that I had to deal with. If I had had a team of people helping me, then perhaps to walk the whole length of the Godavari would have been possible. But I was all alone and I just had to move on.

After getting up, full of good intentions as regards walking and saying goodbye to Satis, my feet again hindered my objective. They simply were not up to it. Leaving it for one more day, seemed the most sensible thing to do. I decided I would look at some local temples and just walking to the temples was an indication that I had made the right decision to rest the feet before I moved on. Just a small walk and it was clear that my feet were unable to carry me that far. On the way to the temple, I had previously seen a man with a sewing machine by the side of the road. I had my ripped trousers with me so I could get them repaired.

The tailor and the owner of the sewing machine spoke surprisingly good English and was happy to help. He was a grandfather and spoke about all his children and any link he could get in concerning the UK, he used with pride. *My daughter this*, and *my son that*. I sat and watched him work. I wondered how long he had been a machinist, but it was obvious by the way he was working that he had been doing it for a very long time. I had no idea how much money I should give this man for fixing my trousers and he seemed more than happy when I gave him 50 rupees, I think he would have been happy taking anything. He was just happy to be speaking to a white person and practising his English. People were passing his shop, seeing me sitting there and this did wonders for his status.

I had almost forgotten the visit to the local temple, and I was quite happy just to sit there, in the man's small shop and let the world pass by. I was in no rush. I had no destination to reach by a certain time, I had no worries about how much water I needed to drink, or how much my feet were hurting. I was relaxed. The man seemed to be enjoying my company so much that he went next door and order lemonade for us both to drink. Soon the lemonade man from next door joined us in the tailor's shop. I say a shop; it was more like a small room and when all three of us found somewhere to sit, the room was full.

Intrigued, they were asking where and why I was in their community and I explained the best I could. Looking at my Google map, they indicated that the next town that I was proposing to walk to tomorrow had no accommodation. I looked at the map and thought, I will worry about that small problem tomorrow. I was enjoying having no worries today and the thought of walking and having nowhere to sleep could just go away for now. I was enjoying my lemonade too much; what will happen tomorrow will happen.

I moved on through the crowds, away from people that wanted to take more selfies and headed for the temple. The temple was small and really not that interesting and after speaking to more locals, I was soon back in my hotel room, ready to sleep. Walking was restarting tomorrow, so I needed to have a good night's sleep. I was still a bit worried that my blisters may not have fully healed and would not be ready for another day's walking.

Over my day with nothing much to worry about, I had done much thinking and I decided that I would be going with Option 2 tomorrow. It was over 40 kilometres to the next town on my route to a place called Newasa. I decided to take a local bus and have it drop me within striking distance of my next accommodation.

I was up at 4.00am and after much confusion, I boarded a bus. I got it to stop about 16 kilometres out of Newasa. I thought that would be a manageable distance to get me used to walking again. Soon it was me, the rucksack and the road once more. After a few hours walking, I arrived at my destination of Newasa, but as the tailor explained yesterday, there was no accommodation, so I had to keep on walking to the next town.

I came to a bridge that crossed the great Godavari River. Being injured, it had been a few days since I had walked by the river. The great river that I was supposed to be following seemed larger than when I had seen it last. I had planned to walk along its banks, but due to safety reasons, this had turned out not to be a good idea, so every time I could get to the river, I was overjoyed just looking at it. As I looked out over the bridge in the distance, I could see someone kayaking. This almost seemed out of place in such a poor area, where no-one seemed to have the time or money for leisure. Any spare time was usually taken up by finding food and shelter.

I followed the road and passed through a small town. It was still early morning; people were smiling and waving at me as I passed by. I found myself following a lady herding donkeys, and because of my sore feet, I struggled to keep up with her pace. After leaving the town, I saw donkeys being milked and the milk was for sale. I thought about trying some, but decided to give it a miss.

I moved on to another small bridge that crossed the river, hoping this would give me a better view downstream. Looking closely, I saw a man walking a donkey onto the river bank, where there seemed to be a large pit dug into the mud (or sand). He pulled the donkey by a rope and tried to get it to go down the pit, but the donkey was having none of it. Stubborn burro, I thought, with a touch of Spanish.

I then started to think about what Satis, the millionaire, had told me; that people eat donkey here. I thought the worst. Was this man pulling this donkey into the pit to kill it and sell the meat? Surely not? I stood watching from the bridge, hoping I was wrong. Soon another donkey was pulled into the pit. I decided it was just a place to get them out of the burning sun. I was just thinking about taking some more photos when two trucks, coming from opposite directions, looked like they would pass each other right where I was standing. I breathed in and leant over the bridge to avoid being hit; one truck just clipped my rucksack. That was close, I thought, then the whole bridge started to wobble. When the trucks had passed, I ran off the bridge to the safety of the road. Indian engineering has never been the same since us Britishers left!

Herding the donkeys

Chapter 13
The Perfect Day

I had been doing a lot of reading about the subconscious mind before I started to walk, so when I woke up in the morning, I believed I had all the answers. Well, I wished it was that easy. Basically, without going into too much detail, I have read a few books and what I understand is that if you can train your subconscious mind to help you plan and make decisions, everyone is a winner. But I am no expert. *'Never stop learning because life never stops teaching'*, was a piece of graffiti I saw on a wall in Mumbai. The principle is that there is so much that is answered by the subconscious mind, without you actually knowing why or how you have come to that decision. For example, you go to bed worried about something and in the morning, you wake up and you feel that you have all the answers.

I read that the best time to train your subconscious mind is just before you go to sleep. I was worried about finding my next accommodation stop, some fifty three kilometres away and I knew that I would not be able to walk that distance in one day. So, did I catch the bus or just walk? When I woke up, the brain said it was time to set off walking.... So that's what I did.

I decided to just walk and see what happened; some people would call this madness. I thought if I could reach the first small settlement which was twenty five kilometres away, I could assess the situation from there. Not once did I stop to question the decision my subconscious mind had made. Not once did the logical part of my brain say '*John, what are you doing? Where are you going to sleep tonight?* Not once did the brain say, '*this is stupid. You know you can't walk fifty three kilometres in one day to make it to the next accommodation'*. But I felt complete confidence with my decision. I was happy to go with my instincts and having no real plan, it didn't worry me at all; if anything, it excited me.

Obviously, I started early and walked for about forty minutes before the sun came up. After an hour's walk, a man stopped on his bike. Every day I face people who really cannot understand why anyone, especially a foreigner wearing a pink hat, should be walking. Each day I have at least five to ten motor bikes stopping, most just wanting a picture, a selfie, with a strange foreigner, but some want to help and give me a lift. I tell them: 'no, I am walking', and I need to walk as much as I can. Annoyingly, the more I walk the more dogs I have to fight away; dogs that are just protecting their territory. I used my blue walking sticks to push the dogs back and keep them from attacking me. The more dogs I faced each day, the more I realised why I loved my cats back home so much.

But one man, Asif, really wanted to help. He was going my way, so admitting to myself that there was no way I could walk fifty three kilometres, I jumped on. He drove, we talked. Soon we stopped and had a chai together. I explained my mission and after this, he followed my blog all the way. He was fascinated that I would want to attempt such a feat on my own and to support the children of India. Another good friend made.

He dropped me off further along the route and now the distance to my accommodation was achievable - only twenty five kilometres. This was still a big walk for me; the most I had done since the second day of my walk. My feet were feeling a little better; well a lot better. I was managing to walk all day, but I was starting to feel that perhaps to walk such a large distance whilst I was still recovering was a bit ambitious. But I was listening to my subconscious mind, so I continued. I joined the river for an hour or so. I walked along its banks for a time, before the terrain became too difficult for me, so I joined the road again.

 This was a treat, seeing the river for two days in a row and I was enjoying the peace and, as I walked along, I felt as though I was being carried by its current. I had initially thought the walk would be like this every day, so when I did get to walk next to the river, I was really appreciative. I soldiered on and it was not too much further on that I saw a school.

I crossed the road, soon surrounded by fifty children. The teacher came out. I explained that I was walking across India for education and he invited me in. But first he checked my passport. I was amazed. I had to show him more evidence that I was real person and my intentions were legitimate. I had no problem with proving that this stranger with a pink hat was actually a teacher on a mission. I commended him for showing such strong safe guarding principles towards his school children. He wanted to see some photos of me, so I showed him the only few that I had of myself and my family, to prove I was not a danger to him or the children. He studied them intensely and when he came to see one of me and my wife holding a glass of champagne, he was shocked. I had not once thought showing a photo of me drinking alcohol would offend. But this was not the only time this same photo caused me embarrassment. He asked what I was drinking, with almost an angry look on his face. I quickly replied apple juice and moved onto the next photo. He nodded with a realisation that, in this case, the truth really didn't matter and could be excused.

The teacher then asked if I could raise some money for his school. I was honest and sadly told him 'no'. There are thousands of schools, not just in India, that need help. This again made me sad. I knew I was helping just a few children in a slum school in Mumbai, but the problems that children and education faces is nationwide and even worldwide.

I felt proud of my small contribution, but realised how small and in some way, insignificant the results of this trip were. I wanted to help everyone: this school, the school I had visited before, but I knew I couldn't. It made me feel worthless, but I was going to keep going however small the difference I was making turned out to be.

Entering the school, I was impressed that it had desks and chairs. The children, as always in India, were so respectful and all wanted to talk to me. I struggled to know who to speak to and who to help. I entered their life for a moment and I didn't know how best to fill my valuable time in this school. I walked around amazed, just talking, looking and smiling. I even wrote my blog address on the board for the teachers to follow my progress.

I was then invited into another classroom to watch children perform a dance they had been learning. The teacher explained the meaning of dance and the song. He told me that we were in an agricultural community. The song was in Marathi and said that if the children kept smiling, then God would provide what they needed for the crops to grow. The sounds and instruments were fantastic to hear. It made such a pleasant change after days of only hearing dogs barking and the sound of the traffic as I walked along the roads.

I was about to leave when I was invited to join in the dance. So, Michael Palin, eat your heart out! Dad Dancing to the rescue and I joined in with the children.

I looked at the playground and wanted to stay and get the skipping ropes out that I had carried with me from the start and introduce some skipping games to these children. This, through my playground business, is how I earn a living back in the UK and I wanted to share this with them. But I knew I couldn't stay too long; it was getting late and I still had two hours of walking ahead of me. To me, this was what the trip was all about; this was one of the main reasons that I had decided to embark on such a trip. I was in a rural school in India; this was what I wanted to see. These are the images of children playing that I could send back to England to all the schools that were following me on my blog. But I knew I had to move on. This made me sad. I wished I could have stayed here all day, but the walking and the hot temperatures would not allow me to do so.

I left the school and hit the road once more. I reached the next town and found good accommodation. All this before 12.30pm. I found that my whole day could be over midday and that was a really strange concept, but I knew after eating, reading and writing my diary, the best thing I needed to do was sleep.

I thought back over the day. I walked twenty five kilometres, even though my feet were paying the price. I saw the Godavari River. I met some great people and I danced in a primary school. The perfect day! Not only was this the perfect day, it had been my favourite so far. Before I set out, I hoped that all the days of my adventure would be like this but, so far, that had not been the case.

Today had given me hope and the will to continue. As I lay in bed, I smiled, looking forward of what new adventures Day 9 would bring.

*A relaxing cup of
chai with Asif*

Chapter 14
A Village, An Ox, A Dam and A Temple

It was an extremely dark morning when I sent off, so a torch was needed. Most mornings, I am up leaving each different hotel so early that I have to wake the guards up who are usually asleep on the floor. As with every other day, it wasn't long before the sun came up and I had walked out of the town and found myself in rural India once more. I was enjoying the walk and I felt lucky to walking in such untouched landscapes. Before long I walked past a small farming village, where I stopped and took some photographs. I was amazed by the small houses these people were living in. I took a closer look and saw straw on the floor. I assumed that all the straw was to soak up all the oxen dung, as I have never seen so many oxen in one place. The villager's homes were plastic huts, coned shaped. The closest thing they resembled would be American Indian tepees. I presumed that it would be impossible to house more than two people in each hut. As I peered through the barbed wire fence, the people on the other side were just going about their every day early morning routines of waking up, stretching outside their huts, cooking on small stoves and toileting themselves in the open air. Maybe the straw was laid on the floor to soak up not just the oxen dung.

I was fascinated. I was like a little boy sticking his head through a hedgerow, watching hares' box in a field for the first time. I was so desperate to get in through the hole in the fence and introduce myself, but I didn't want to shock or surprise these people. It wasn't fair for a complete stranger to just invite themselves into their world.

But it must have been my lucky day, for as I was taking the photos, a young man waved me over. I accepted and soon found myself on the other side of the fence, inside the farming village. With no English, I managed to find out that these people were sugar cane farmers. I was invited to eat with them and drink chai, so I did. It made me think of all those travel programs I had watched on the TV and made me wonder how much of the filming was pre-planned. This one certainly wasn't. I walked around, shaking people's hands, trying to say the odd word in Hindi to make me feel more accepted.

I tried to explain my journey and showed the golden ticket that explained my mission, but no one could read. One woman just said 'no school'. The same woman asked me to join her sitting on the straw outside her hut. She wanted to make me tea and feed me grain. I accepted and just took my rucksack off, leant back and smiled. The lady boiled the water on a handmade fire, in a pan and then added the chai. She was so welcoming and happy.

It made me think of all the new people that I have met over the years and how they first invite you into their home, pouring you a wine or a beer, sharing a drink to get to know you. This was so much more powerful. No English was exchanged and yet I was welcomed into her home. No fancy home to show off, no fancy car parked in the drive way, just people, company, shelter, food and friendliness.

Sitting outside a hut, drinking tea, I could have sat there for hours, soaking up this new experience, but realising I had a whole day of walking ahead of me, (despite having all the time in the world, ironically I had no time to stay), I had to move on. For the first time, I almost resented the walking, thinking it was getting in the way of all these wonderful new experiences. Then I thought if I wasn't walking and was, instead, travelling by bus or train, I would never have stumbled across such a place. But I had a real rethink at this moment. I had embarked on this trip, mainly knowing that it was going to be a physical challenge.

But because of the situations that I had experienced, especially over the last two days, this trip was so much more than just the physical challenge of walking across India.

I was a traveller and I had always enjoyed finding out first-hand about people's cultures and here was my chance staring me in the face.

Should I calm down and be easier on myself? Should I stop beating myself up with this walking stuff and just live in the moment? Enjoy these wonderful encounters I had been given the chance to see and experience or should I forget them, move on, just concentrate on the walking and get to the other side? I had a feeling I would wrestle with this dilemma for the entire trip.

I was just about to get up and leave when the man, who initially invited me into the village, pointed to an ox cart. There were three oxen – two in the front and one behind. He climbed up onto the cart and pointed for me to join him. I know I was supposed to be walking, but I couldn't resist, so I jumped on board! I was like a prince leaving his city behind. I shouted good bye as the cart moved slowly out of the village. We hit the road. I sat back and smiled. He controlled the beasts with clicking and blowing sounds to make them change direction. I had nearly twenty kilometres to walk ahead of me and I think he was prepared to take me all the way. I was enjoying the moment but I felt like I was cheating, but being carried along by oxen on the road side was an opportunity I was not going to turn down. I just thought, how did this happen?

Maybe ten minutes later, a man walking along the same road, overtook us. I knew then it was time to get off this cart and start walking again! I knew that we were travelling slowly, but slower than someone walking. I couldn't believe it. I managed to get him to stop. I asked him to take a photo while I held the reins. I didn't realise, but as I was posing for the photo, I was actually pulling the reins and the ox started to walk backwards. The oxen walked backwards down the same road we had just walked on. I would have loved someone to have videoed this moment. I can imagine my face would have said all that needed to be said. To say I was a bit worried would have been an understatement, and I called the farmer for help. I even started producing my own whistles and clicks, but that just increased the beasts' pace and I was holding on for dear life. The owner ran after us and soon rescued what could have been a real embarrassing moment. He smiled and regained control. Then he shook my hand and asked for nothing, but I gave him 300 rupees, (around £3.20). He took my money and smiled. This was probably more than he earns in a week. I don't think he wanted any money, but it was one of those situations where if you give, you feel like you have been given.

After walking for nearly four hours, it was time to stop and doctor my feet. This was something you know that I need to do at least twice, sometimes more, during the course of a walking day. Change my socks, let my feet breathe, change the plasters and apply talcum powder, deodorant and Vaseline. I was sitting down, going through the motions and, as usual, was soon surround by people watching what can only be described as for them, a crazy occurrence. While this was going on, a man turned up that could speak English. I told him what I was doing and he explained my journey to the on looking crowd. He told me that he was a photographer for the local media. His name was Satis. Another Satis, I thought to myself. He told me that his name meant '*satisfied*'. I was meeting so many people so quickly that were helping me on my journey that I couldn't keep up.

We exchanged numbers. He understood my mission and bought me water and chai. He told me that I should walk along the path, not the road, to Paithan, the next town, as it ran past the 2nd biggest dam in India – the *Jayakwadi Dam*. This was the first dam in India to supply power. It is part of one the largest irrigation projects in Maharashtra, with its water being mainly used to irrigate agricultural land in Marathwada, the drought-prone region of the state. It also provides water for drinking and industrial usage to nearby towns and villages and also to the districts of Aurangabad and Jalna.

The surrounding area of the dam has a garden and a bird sanctuary. [4] It is also fed by the Godavari River, so I was eager to be seeing the river again.

It felt really good to be walking on a path and not a road and, after thirteen kilometres, I reached the dam. It was huge and the lake feeding into the river was so expansive, it looked like the sea. I walked on over a bridge where I could see both the dam and the Godavari at the same time. In the distance, I saw people digging in the sand. They were looking for anything valuable to sell, possibly even coins. Everyone was so busy foraging that they took no notice of me and I enjoyed not be stared at. It looked like a scene out of archeologically program; I have never ever seen so many people excavating at the same time. But later I found out they were digging for survival and some people did this as their only form of income. They would be digging all day and every day.

I continued along and I could see there was an easy path down to the river, so I walked down and touched the water of the great Godavari. From the distance, it looked like people were swimming, but as I moved closer, that was not the case. Here, too, people were busy working; this time they were panning the river to find anything valuable. The last time I had seen anyone panning a river was years ago in the US where people were panning for gold.

You know, one of those false situations where people, including myself, pan the river and think we are back in time, during the days of the civil war, where land was free and so was the gold – if you were lucky enough to find any. But here people were not panning for fun they were panning for survival and hoping that today they would pan something that was valuable enough they could trade it for food.

When I looked into the river, I could see all sorts of things that had been washed up. But the thing that amazed me the most were the stone statues. Broken faces from old temple statues just lying on the river bank or bobbing up and down in the river.

Looking and touching these statues, I wondered where they had come from and how old they were. Just as I was admiring these pieces of art history, a fight broke out on the river bank. One of the young men had sieved up something valuable in the river. Everyone ran after him and he moved further into the river to get away from them. They all wanted what he had found. I just looked on with total amazement. This then hit home the real seriousness of the panning. It was panning to survive and someone had found something valuable and everyone wanted it and, more importantly, were prepared to fight for it.

It reminded me of a wildlife programme on the plains, where the lioness kills her prey and the hyenas move in to try and steal it. She has to fight off all the attackers. Only then can it be claimed for herself and eaten.

After the fight, I returned to looking into the great river. It made me think that surely these abandoned stone statues must be worth more than the odd coin. But, out of respect for their religion, these people would not dream of moving these items. These broken artefacts which, to my untrained eye, looked valuable, would remain there in the river looking on every day, while these poor people fought over finding an odd coin that could provide their next meal.

I needed to move on. I had a final look down the great river, and hoped I'd be able to see it again soon. Shortly after, I reached the town and found a hotel. I was given a full menu and shown into a bar and asked if I wanted a beer. Before I even could think about my answer, I said no. I had not once wanted a beer. I just couldn't face the risk of a headache or feeling dehydrated in this heat. This was definitely an out-of-character approach for me, because drinking beer is one of my favourite past times, but this was not a normal situation I was in and my brain had taken over my heart. If my heart had made the decision, I would have been on my second beer before I had found a seat.

After a full morning's walking on top of getting up at 4.30am, I am not usually fit for much else, but Satis phoned. He wanted to meet up, so despite my tiredness, I agreed. He turned up at my hotel with his daughter.

As with the first Satis, the millionaire, this Satis wanted to take me sight-seeing. My feet were really not up to much but he convinced me. We walked through a busy market, avoiding the strolling cows and soon found ourselves at a huge temple, the Eknath Maharaj Temple. Shoes were taken off and we went inside. As Satis was a photographer, he asked the people that were chanting and singing if it was alright for me to join them. It was, so I did. I sat uncomfortably on the floor feeling like I was a real part of their culture.

We walked outside and, as the temple was situated on the banks of the river, I was able to see the Godavari again, this time at sunset.
Another moment where I felt lucky to experience this beautiful sight. This was a special place because of the river flowing past it; it had been rolling past this magnificent temple for years and I was there to witness it.

We took a slow walk back to the hotel. I grabbed my dinner – two samosas - and said goodbye to yet another great person. Satis (and his daughter), jumped back on his bike and waved goodbye. I hope we can stay in touch.

Maybe I should have had that beer after all. No, I didn't want it and I certainly didn't need it!

Satis, with his daughter

Chapter 15
The Road to Nowhere

Every day is different, I get that. Some are better than others, I get that. Some days, so much happens in one day that it feels like five days in one. But at other times, the time just drags on. This is a long walk and at times, that's really all it is; one giant hike across India.

If I was to say I was not bored during this walk then I would not be being truthful. Most of the time I was in far too much pain to be bored, but sometimes the road just seemed to go on and on, with not too much to see. People stopping to ask if they can help made the days go quicker, but when no one stopped and you had no human contact, it was just a personal battle with yourself. A battle where you don't know if you are winning or losing, but a battle you must continue to fight. A mind battle in 50° C is not a battle you want to keep fighting for too long. Eventually, you could go completely mad.

This morning, tiredness was starting to rear its head and my shoulders were killing me. I had concentrated so much on my feet since the start of the trip I hadn't really had time to think about the rest of my body. Each morning, the shock of lifting the rucksack amazed me. It was so heavy to lift I was astounded that I managed to walk with it for six to seven hours every day. Each morning I braced myself raising the rucksack up to the same height as my body, using the bed for support, before slipping it on.

The next accommodation was thirty five kilometres away and I knew I would have to jump a bus some of the distance, as covering this on foot in one day would be impossible. Walking through deep rural India, the gap between each accommodation was getting further and further apart.

I had worked out that if I caught the bus and got the driver to drop me in the middle of nowhere, I could walk to the next night's accommodation. I asked the bus conductor to stop the bus in Takali Ambad, which was nothing more than a few shacks by the side of the road. The conductor thought I was insane and couldn't understand why I would want to get off the bus in the middle of fields. I didn't bother trying to explain that.

I thought that if I could walk somewhere between fifteen and twenty five kilometres every day, the trip could still be achievable. This would mean I could still walk every day and, in my head, this kept me going. Obviously, the fact I was not walking all the way (due to lack of accommodation, having no tent and my decision not to risk sleeping alone outside with the leopards), would not go away. But I had no option if I wanted to complete this trip in some shape or form; this was the method that I would have to adopt.

Leaving the bus, I started to walk the remaining nineteen kilometres which I knew I could achieve before the sun became too dangerously hot to walk in. But for the first time so far, after looking at the map, I had other important issues to worry about.

The terrain was so remote that, for the first time, I had to think hard about how I could get water. Usually I have no problem as there are many roadside shacks that I can visit whilst walking and top up my water supply. But on this day, I was worried; there just seemed to be nowhere where I could get water. I had worked out during my walking that I would consume a minimum of one litre for every hour of walking (this also included having rehydration salts mixed in with the water).

When the walk began, I was very careful not to drink too much. I was carrying only two litres of water with me, so I knew I would need water after two to three hours and I knew I had to walk, with stops, for at least five hours. Most people would undoubtedly say that this was complete madness and it probably was. But somehow, I always thought that I would be ok, that someone would help me, or on the unknown road there would be a place where I could get water, so stubbornly I marched on.

After about an hour of walking, my shoulders had toughened up, but my feet had got worse, they were certainly worse than yesterday. My right foot had developed another blister, and I was limping. I knew that this was no way to continue and with the amount of weight I was carrying, I was aware that this limping could cause further injury. I knew that I would most probably be over compensating to accommodate the limping and I was worried I could pull a muscle. I felt alone. Whilst walking, I tried not to look at how much distance I had covered as this just made it harder. I did this once and continually looking at my phone to see what distance I had walked just depressed me and made me feel really slow. Instead, I just timed my walking every day. I knew I had to be walking for between five to seven hours (minus the stops) and so I would just keep an eye on how long I had been walking, rather than the distance I had covered.

Another personal mind battle, one that I was not sure I was winning, but looking at the time rather than the distance did seem to be helping in some strange way.

I passed a small village where I saw some children playing cricket, but other than that, I saw nothing except roads and fields; all the time my water supplies were getting lower. An elderly man who, I would guess by looking at him, was in his seventies, joined me walking, but I struggled to keep up with him and soon he turned left, waving good bye. I managed, at last, to find a small shack that sold water and on I walked. I was aiming to get to a place called Shahgadh and, after a really hard, lonely day, I arrived.

As I walked into the town, it looked very industrial and I was hoping there would be somewhere I could sleep. I asked several people and they all said that this town had no overnight accommodation. Google had misinformed me. It was 11.00am and the temperature was 48°C. I knew after nearly six hours walking that if I couldn't sleep here in this town, I would have to move onto the next. I knew to walk it would be impossible. I was directed by the people to yet another bus station and I was left with no other option but to catch a bus to the next town, Georai.

I arrived in Georai and soon found a hotel. I was completely shattered; blisters and shoulders killing me and just all round exhausted. blisters and shoulders killing me and just all round exhausted. During the day, my trusty rucksack had developed its second spilt, so however tired I was, I knew I had to sort this problem out before I could rest for the day.

Luck was on my side and the owner of the hotel helped me. '*I am on a mission from God*', like the phrase from the Blue Brothers film, but I truly was.

 I am not a religious person, but I thought there must be someone helping me get across to the other side.

The owner of the hotel took me to his friend next door who, with his machine, sewed the spilt, again for something like 10 pence. I thank him and returned to my hotel. I bought some bananas (which is all I seemed to eat), and collapsed in my hotel room. Two hours later, I did venture out after I had mended my body and washed my clothes in a bucket. I needed something more substantial to eat apart from just bananas, so I was out in the street looking for a meal. This, after a long day on the road, can prove to be very difficult, with the language barrier often being the biggest obstacle.

A restaurant was soon found and, in broken Hindi and English, I managed to order a vegetable curry. It nearly blew my head off with the amount of spices it contained, especially after I had ordered it with 'zero spice'.

 I thought I would be safe, but I wasn't. I managed to eat it and said good bye to the owner and cook of the restaurant (one in the same person). Walking out in the street, on my short stroll back to the hotel, my head was nearly blown off, this time due to the heat and not the spices.

It was 51°C; it was so dry and hot, I felt like the inside of my mouth was burning more than it was after the curry I had just eaten. I hadn't experienced heat like it before; it felt like my eyebrows and eye lids were catching fire. Despite the pain in my feet, the stroll turned into a run back to the hotel.

That was day ten finished with.

The Road to Nowhere

Chapter 16
A Dentist, a Lorry Driver, No Menu, Just Food

It was my wife Michelle's birthday and this was the first time since we have been married that I had not shared the day with her. I thought of her all day and hoped I would get a chance to speak to her later on.

The same problem was there again; the next accommodation was too far for me to walk to. I was up at 5.00am, waking the hotel guard to let me out. Walking to the bus station, I started to think that this would be the pattern for the rest of my trip. It was a one kilometre walk to the station and I had planned to hop on a bus and get it to stop twenty kilometres from the town where I knew I could find somewhere to sleep. I was now coming to terms with this and becoming more accepting of the situation, knowing this was the only safe way I could manage to walk every day. After yesterday's long day's walking, I felt surprisingly good. The blister was doubly taped up and my shoulders, I thought, were just getting used to the weight. I had done no training for this walk, so I knew the first two weeks would be hard until the body got used to what it had to go through every day. I was getting fitter on the job. When I got to the bus station, I had the same language problems trying to communicate with anyone who could direct me towards the correct bus, the one that was going where I wanted to go.

I found that by writing the name of a place down on a scrap of paper, I was more easily understood. I realised after communicating with as many as five different people that the bus that I need to catch didn't leave for another hour and half. I looked at my map and then realised that if I didn't leave until 7.00am, I would be struggling to be able to walk to my destination, because it would be approaching mid-day and that is not a time where you want to be out walking.

A man approached, speaking really good English and it turned out that he was going to the same place as me, a place called Malegaon. I knew as soon as I met him that he was going to help me; lady luck was on my side. I explained my mission and the problems I was having finding accommodation, hence the reason I was travelling on the bus. He looked at my mapped route and suggested I change it. I was all ears; no plans meant exactly that. He suggested I stay in another town, one next to the river. According to my map, this town didn't offer accommodation, but he assured me that it did; he then wrote down the name of the hotel I should stay in and sketched me a map. When we boarded the bus, we spoke in more detail. I found out that his name was Dr. Lohiya Rajesh, a dentist, travelling by bus to get back to see his family after working each week miles away from where he lived.

I thought back to all the people that had helped me so far on the trip and the difference in their occupations was so varied. Before I left the bus, he phoned a friend and arranged for him to meet me when I got off the bus, to walk me to the hotel that he had recommended. I was amazed by the kindness of the people in this country, but he wasn't finished there. He knew that I was on this trip for charity, helping underprivileged children in India and he wanted to contribute. He offered me money, but I refused. So, when the bus came to my stop, he paid my fare. We shook hands, and said that his friend would meet me once I had walked my twenty kilometres into town. After walking by the side of the road for about forty five minutes, I came across a huge sugar factory. A silver monster that you could smell; the smell reminded me of being back home in Suffolk, driving past the sugar factory in Bury St. Edmunds. As I walked on, I knew that I had to move quickly, as the heat increased considerably the closer it came to midday. People were stopping me all the time, wanting to take selfies with me. Most days that is just part of the norm, but today I was worried. I still had five hours walking in front of me and these stoppages were delaying my progress. Again, it was a moment where the need to move on was getting in the way of me enjoying the present. This day alone four bikes, one jeep and two cars had stopped, offering me a lift. They couldn't understand when I refused their kind offers.

Finally, after four and half hours of walking I approached the great Majalgaon Dam. It was enormous and as I approached it, the water it held back looked more like a sea.

This dam was constructed in 1976 and crosses the Sindhaphana River, a major tributary of the Godavari. This was the second dam I had seen, although this one seemed larger. It was like the first dam in that it was fed by the Godavari, so I could say I was walking along my planned route of following the Godavari River, just as my dentist friend had advised me earlier on the bus.

As I continued, I saw a large gathering of teenagers and they were all very excited; I had to investigate. It seemed that they had just caught a huge fish from the dam; one boy was proudly showing it off. I knew I had over an hour to go before I reached my accommodation, but I couldn't help but stop and get a photograph of me holding the fish.

Leaving the boys with the fish and walking away from the dam to follow a dusty path leading into town, I saw something else that I knew I had to investigate. The temperature was approaching 50°C degrees, but even though it was nearly midday, I was sure I had the energy to keep me going. Just to the side of the path was a large dusty open space and there were some children playing cricket.

This was my big chance to join in on their game. I approached the young boys whose ages ranged from seven to twelve and asked if I could join in. They accepted and were excited that a white man would want to join in their game. First, I batted and managed to hit a couple of fours, but there were edges off the bat that would have been stopped if there were enough players to employ a third man. Then it was time to turn my arm over; I was hit all over the place. I thought I was bowling fast until a boy about ten came down the wicket and hit straight over my head for a six. It was time to stop. I took some photos, shook the boys' hands and went back to walking on the dusty path.

When I entered the town, more and more people approached me and asked if I needed help. Shaking my head, I thanked them and continued to walk into town, following the dentist's hand written map. Closer to the town, the traffic started to build up so I knew I must be near the centre and the bus station, where the recommended hotel would be waiting for me.

A man on a bike, with his wife and baby daughter behind him, stopped me on the road. I didn't think anything of it, as I had been stopped so many times already during the course of the day. But this man was really over friendly, almost as if he knew me. Then he spoke: 'Dr. Rajesh asked me to meet you and show you to your hotel'.

I had almost forgotten that my dentist friend had made the phone call to arrange this, it seemed so long ago, yet it had only happened earlier that same day. I was shocked by these people's generosity. The man on the bike then told his wife and daughter to get off the bike and wait by the side of the road, while he ran me to the suggested hotel. I felt embarrassed, but it was already organised and I wasn't about to refuse. However, I did feel bad that his wife and child were simply abandoned by the side of the road, just to help me. So, on yet another bike - this time delivering me straight to the hotel. He then came with me into the hotel to make sure that I was given the best room and the best rate. I thanked the man that had helped me on the bike and he smiled; I assumed he returned to his wife and daughter that he had left by the roadside.

When I checked into the room and went about my daily cleaning chores, I found that, for the first time, I had hot water. Yippee! I went out into the street to buy my bananas and salt to soak my feet. I managed to find somewhere to eat and, for a large vegetable curry with roti and three litres of water to take away, all came to 85 rupees, the equivalent of £1.00. I was ready for bed, and it was only 4,00pm, but not without a hot shower first, I couldn't wait to feel the hot water on my skin. Even though the temperature outside was in in the 50s, it is surprising how much you miss hot water when you can't get it. But disaster struck.

The water was so hot I couldn't get under it and there was only hot water available, I had waited this long for hot water and now I had no cold. How ironic, and only in India.

====

The next morning was really no different from any other morning, except sometimes I felt happier and more mentally strong than I had done on previous days. This day I didn't. Today, the walking was like a job or a chore, something that had to be done every day. It felt like someone had given me a prison sentence and my punishment on remand was to walk across India.

As I walked, I thought about reading the book *Tom Sawyer*, and for a punishment, he had to paint a long fence, where he couldn't see the end of, but he still had to keep going. That old cliché of you can't eat an elephant all at once; you have to eat one chunk at a time, kept popping into my head. When I hear that saying, I always think who would eat an elephant anyway? My walking was bit by bit and if I studied the map in great detail, it would depress me. The distance I had covered so far looked so insignificant, with the largest distance to cover still ahead of me, so I decided that I would not look at the whole of the map of India, well, not until I was somewhere near the other end.

Every morning as I walked, I was surprised at how many people were active at such an early time, but now I was getting used to it. I suppose their situation was no different from mine. They had to get all their work done before the sun made it too hot to work. I walked and finally came to the river again, but today it looked dirty and sad. I marched on, taking the advice from the dentist that the town I was approaching was a great place to stay and it had accommodation. But as I approached the town, I wasn't so sure. Many bikes stopped, offering me lift to anywhere I wanted to go. I refused, but as the day moved on, the more tempted I was to say *yes*, and just jump on the next available lift to speed my arrival at the nearest town.

But I stayed strong, refusing, put my head down and continued on walking. I saw some children playing, I approached them and, for the first time ever, they ran away. That didn't help to boost my spirits. However, one girl, braver than the others, stayed as I came closer. She was carrying a large jug on her head which looked to be almost half the size of her body. She let me take a photo and joined me walking for a while. I assumed she was just carrying fresh water and she must have been no older than seven.

Approaching the town, I had the feeling that this place would not have any accommodation and I was proved right. This was a regular problem, both Google maps, and people's recommendations have both proved to be wrong. This town had nowhere for me to sleep.

Again, I knew I was in trouble. I had now been walking about twenty kilometres and for nearly six hours. I referred to my map and it was another eight kilometres to the next town. As usual, the sun was getting hotter. I thought if I make it to the next town today that could injure me and stop my progress for walking the day after. But I was stuck. Thinking like this, I was going to give up and take a ride to the next town, even though I knew I couldn't walk the whole distance across my planned route, I still didn't want to cheat myself at every opportunity. More bikes stopped, more selfies taken and more lifts refused.

Once again, I was saved. Walking over a bridge, a middle age man, who introduced himself as Habil, just started to walk with me. He didn't speak much English but wanted to communicate, telling me he was a lorry driver from Mumbai. He then started to name all the districts in Mumbai and I joined in his game, naming nearly as many as him. He was impressed and knew that I came from Mumbai, his home town. He smiled; we had something in common and, yet again, I had made a new friend. He then told he was driving back to Mumbai tomorrow and did I want a lift? I laughed and a part of me wanted to say yes, and call this mad trip off for good. But I declined and I tried to explain to him about my mission and I think he understood why I said no to his kind offer.

I wondered, after walking for about thirty minutes with Habil, why is walking with me? Was he just keeping me company? I knew I had about five kilometres still to go before I reached the next town. As we walked along, we crossed a huge bridge spanning the Godavari and Habil took some photos of me.

It was on this bridge that he called in the help. Walking along, Habil was forever looking behind me to see what vehicles were coming past. Then he stepped into the middle of the road, put his arm out and stopped a massive truck that was approaching us. I didn't really understand what he was doing, and there was a moment when I thought the truck would not be able to stop in time. But it did. He communicated with the driver and the next thing I knew; he was lifting me up into this massive truck. How could I refuse? I just climbed up inside the cab. Ever since I arrived in India, I had wanted to ride in one of these brightly decorated trucks and now was my chance. The last time I had been in a truck was when I was hitchhiking across Australia, but that was thirty years ago. I couldn't believe how far these trucks were above the ground. Once I was in, Habil struggled to lift my rucksack into the cab. He then jumped up himself. He said in broken English, '*if you won't let me take you back to your family in Mumbai, then at least let me take you to the next town*'. Many times, before, I smiled to myself and thought if I wanted to make a story up, it could have never been as unbelievable as what was actually happening to me now and every day of this trip so far.

Less than five minutes later, the truck stopped and Habil
indicated for me to get down. We had only moved two
kilometres nearer to my destination and, again, I was not sure
what was happening or where I was going.

Habil pointed to an iron looking shed. I was in his capable
hands, I hoped. I looked, suddenly realising that Habil had
taken me to his home. We said thank you and goodbye to the
truck driver. I presume that all truckers have a code and
everyone helps each other out, because it seemed to me that
Habil really didn't know the driver that well.

His home was more like a garage but he invited me inside.
There were two beds and a place to make food and chai; that
was it. Habil introduced me to his friend who spoke even less
English than Habil, so he made the chai. He explained that
this was his home when he was working on the road and not
with his family back in Mumbai. I was offered a seat on one of
the beds, and enjoyed the company. Habil was soon on the
phone and three more of his friends came around to see me.
The *Golden Ticket* explaining my mission was shared again
and everyone just wanted to shake my hand and have their
photo taken. Habil then led me from his home to a piece of
land at the back of the iron garage. There he and his friend
were growing their own vegetables to eat. I had always
wondered why the India people were starving when there was
so much land to go around and it took a lorry driver to show
the population how to be self-sufficient and survive.

One of Habil's friends offered to take me into the town, but I refused and decided to walk. I thanked Habil so much for his kindness and we exchanged phone numbers.

The familiar pattern was followed again, of me struggling into town, like a tired lost gun fighter. People looked out of their window as someone new approached their town, but this one was not about to start a gun fight, he just wanted a bed. Finally I found a hotel; it was really dirty and had no power when I arrived, but it felt safe so I wasn't about to start walking the streets to look for a better cleaner alternative. I accepted where I was shown, and in the darkness, I could just make out graffiti on the walls. It was less than £3.00 for the night, but I knew that all I had to do was wash, sleep and then move on tomorrow.

But with the lack of power, that wasn't that easy and with no fan, the heat was tremendous. I looked around and realised that the floor was filthy, so I couldn't walk around bare footed. After having a cold-water bucket shower, I was worried about getting more infection in my newly formed blisters.
I ventured downstairs to try to find somewhere where I could eat. The young boy who had first shown me the room sat in a reception area, with another couple, who I thought could be his mother and father.

 I gestured that I needed to eat and they indicated for me sit down and they would make something here. I thought about asking where the menu was, but realised that was not the sort of place that would have a menu. So I sat, waiting to see what I was going to be served. The father went off to prepare the food, and a vegetable curry appeared. So, no menu, just food and it was pleasant enough and cost no more than 80 pence. I thanked them all and returned to my powerless room.

With some people like Prekash, a friend is someone you need; with Habil, a friend is someone you have!

Leaving Mumbai

The start of the great Godavari River

The first of many carcasses by the side of the road

Dairy churns outside of my Nashik accommodation

Prekash's family in the kitchen

The first school I visited on the walk

Donkeys on the banks of the Godavari

Making tea in the ox village

And me drinking it– ah, chai!

A ride on an ox cart

The Jayakwadi Dam – the second largest dam in India

A game of cricket? And why not

India is cricket and cricket is India

Life on the road

Receiving a blessing at the Shanti Project

Off the train, and walking again

All the villagers turned out to see the stranger at Sharad's house

Making dhosas in the street – the best breakfast I had all trip

A man selling goats' head. I think I'll give that a miss

A street vendor, selling mainly sweets

The great river, though not looking at its best

My good friend, Naresh, washing my clothes – his feet were his tools

SV in his friend's shop, where you could buy anything – as long as it was made of plastic!

Fame at last! We made the local newspaper

Tree juice anyone?

This lady had her hands full

Drying my nylon socks ready for the next day's walking

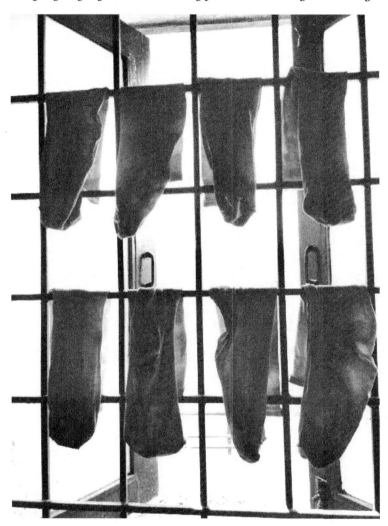

The great Godavari River in full flow

Saying goodbye to Johnny

Sandgrounders, hard at work. People from my wife's hometown of Southport also go by this name. But here on the Godavari, it could not be more different.

Time for one last game of cricket

The Obelisk Tower in Yanam and the end of the adventure

Chapter 17
LB, Sarang, Lata and the Shanti Project

I woke this morning to a power cut, so packing the rucksack and pampering the feet took so much longer than normal. It was all done by torchlight. I was ready and just about to walk out of the hotel when the power came back on. Oh well, let's just walk.

It was a sixteen kilometres walk today and my feet were not feeling too bad. I have learnt to never get over confident, because I know it won't be long before a new blister develops.

Walking on the road side, you obviously have to be very careful of the traffic. In most parts of the world, the rule of thumb is to always walk facing the oncoming traffic, but not in India.

Cars, trucks, tractors and any other vehicle you can think of all believe they have the power to over (or under) take. This means if you walk with your back to the traffic, you can't face the over-taking cars coming from the opposite direction. I have found the overtaking cars to be the most dangerous, so it is those I decided to face. At times, they are so keen to over-take that they leave the road and come on to the dirt on the side of the road where I am usually walking on.

After nearly completing my target walk for the day, another
slightly older man stopped on his bike. I know he is not
interested in a selfie. We talked and I don't know why I
decided to take his help and jumped on his bike. But, I am so
glad I did. We drove off but after only fifty meters he stopped
and pulled into a roadside shack. 'Shall we have some tea?' he
asked and I thought, 'why not?'

We were not there long before LB, another great friend to be,
told all the people in the shack about my quest. They all shook
my hand and all the tea was free. A man approached me and
gave me his sunglasses. Earlier when I was walking, I thought
to myself this could just be one of those quiet days where
nothing much would happen; but how wrong could I have
been.

LB got on the phone; he told me he knew someone that lived
in the town, Parbhani that would look after me. He said he was
sure he would love to meet me. It was only a two kilometres
walk to town and I insisted I would walk there. I was just
leaving when LB's phone rang. He gave it to me. The man on
the other end of the phone spoke perfect English and told me
not to book a lodgings but instead, have LB bring me to his
house. So, I did. Back on the bike and soon I was at the house
of Sarang and Lata. I was greeted and blessed into their home.

Talking, I found out that Sarang was a social worker and was doing all sorts of things for charity. It was like we had met before. I sat in his house and we exchanged stories. As I looked this man straight in the eye, I could only see kindness and caring; his large rimmed blackish glasses just magnified this impression. He wore a impressive handle bar moustache and this highlighted his smile and his friendly openness. This person cared, not about money, not about any job or any career, he just cared for people and yes, I could tell this from having just met him.

Lata, Sarang's wife, was friendly, supportive and kind just like her husband. She was small in stature and as I looked her, I could see her looking warmly at Sarang: it was obvious they had a caring relationship. She spoke gently, but when she spoke everyone in the room stopped and listened. She had a presence and an influence not just here in her house, but on a much wider spectrum. Later, my opinion of her was proved correct by the influence she held in the charity she ran and organised. She balanced the way Sarang worked and her warmth gave off more than that: she gave her heart and everything she believed in, with an unassuming hidden, but strong passion. She, like Sarang, truly cared.

Showing me my room, I was impressed; it was vast and took up the whole of the top floor of their town house. Fate, I was thinking, there must be someone looking over me. How can I keep being this lucky?

Feeding me breakfast, they arranged an agenda for me for the day. Usually after the walk in the morning, my day is finished, but on this occasion, it had only just begun. Sarang explained that he and Lata were helping run something called the *Shanti Project* [5]. This was a local project set up by an orphan girl, Shanti, who had been adopted by German parents. She later returned to India to try to find her biological mother, but was unsuccessful. Lata witnessed this search and owning land in the town, decided to help Shanti establish herself and the project was formed. Nowadays, money is raised to support women in similar circumstances to stop them abandoning their children. The project's main aim is to give women a role in society where they can earn their own independent money.

I was to be given a tour around all aspects of the project but before we left the house, Sarang had a problem with his car - the battery had gone flat. Whilst we were waiting for it to be fixed, I was shown the downstairs of their house. This was where Sarang's mother lived and she invited me in. Sarang's mother was blind and I sat with her while Sarang's sister-in-law made us some tea.

The downstairs was old fashioned in style, but scrupulously clean; there were ornaments and photographs on every wall and the place looked like it had remained untouched for thirty years. Conversation was difficult, as I sat on a huge sofa, my legs dangling because they couldn't reach the floor. But with odd word of Hindi and the odd word of English we managed to communicate and I believe this old lady could sense my good intentions. She thought I was just like her son and I had chosen to work for free. I felt so relaxed sitting there, again entering someone's life for such a small time and trying to understand that not everyone's life is easy. But on many occasions, just like this one, it can be very enjoyable. There were moments of silence but not once did it seem uncomfortable. I could have sat dangling my legs from that sofa all day.

Two men turned up outside the house and recharged the battery. Sarang had paid for these people to restart his car. Later I asked him about the service and he said that these people earn a living going round to cars that won't start, recharging the batteries. Like a privatised RAC, I thought.

Once the car was working again, Sarang, Lata and I drove to Lata's office, where I was given water and told more about the *Shanti Project*. I was all ears and just wished I could stay with these people for a bit longer and help them with their charity work.

But I knew that wasn't possible as I had to keep moving, but I was still determined to see as much as I could in the time I had with them.

The next stop was just a small drive to the hospital; the same hospital where Shanti was born. This was my first experience visiting a local Indian hospital. The first thing that I was blown away by was the smell, and to be honest, it wasn't a smell you could call hygienic. It was a maternity hospital and I was informed that sixty children are born here every day. Without being too graphic, there was a distinctive smell that reminded me that we were mammals and the smell was, in a way, similar to that you might smell in a zoo. It took my breath away for all the wrong reasons.

I was allowed in after signing a form and soon found myself in one of the many maternity rooms. I met a lady who had given birth her daughter only four hours previously; she let me hold her. I spoke to the father who was a farm labourer, who told Sarang that he earned less than 50000 rupees a year, (£500). We stayed with the family for about ten minutes and I noticed that not once had the mother stopped crying. I remember back to my own experience when my children were born and could not remember my wife Michelle crying the way this woman was.

But I just put it down to the fact that everyone's experience of child birth is very different. Lata then spoke to the woman and found out that she was crying so much because she had given birth to a daughter and not a son. This made me tremendously sad.

Leaving the hospital, I was driven to the red-light district. Another part of the *Shanti Project* is to get women working, sewing and making things to sell to discourage them from going into prostitution. Within ten minutes, I had gone from a hospital to a brothel. I met some of the women who were pleased to see us and we spoke to them for some time. I told Sarang that since living in India, I had not seen many signs of prostitution. He answered that the more it is hidden, the worse it is. I agreed and we walked up the street where the shacks that these women had to use for their work were situated; they could only be described as disgusting. They were wooden in construction and looked more like stables than a brothel. It was very sad.

Sarang then took me up an alley way which was connected to the main strip; the huts there were in an even worse condition. Sarang wanted to find one particular girl that he was very worried about. This girl, about thirteen years of age, was the daughter of one of the prostitutes in the area. He was worried that due to family's lack of money, she would be following in her mother's footsteps.

He then went on to tell me the real truth behind why he was particularly worried about this girl.

We found her in one of the huts. Sarang explained that she was a virgin and that was a worrying time for the young girl. It seemed that the mother had left her alone and was nowhere to be seen. Sarang had seen this situation before and he wanted to help. He described how rich men from the Middle East fly to India specifically to have sex with a virgin, paying in the region of 70,000 rupees (over £700), for the privilege. That is a lot of money here in India; this is big business. When we left, the girl remained alone in her hut. Sarang was extremely upset and shed a tear. He just looked me straight in the face, telling me that there was nothing he could do to stop this inevitable situation. I agreed that it seemed terrible and reassured him that there seemed to be little anyone could do about this underworld black market behaviour.

This wonderful charity encourages the next generation of women not to go down the prostitution route. To lighten the mood, I was then shown all the sewing workshops that have been set up for these women to work in and earn their own money. I visited three separate locations; one was even in a slum area. Each time, I received a blessing on entering the properties. In total, I was blessed four times in one day and given flowers and a wreath. What a day. I couldn't believe how much I had enjoyed entering into the lives of these people.

We wanted to go to a local school, as I had planned to get some skipping ropes out and play some playground games with the children. But unfortunately, the school was closed by the time we got there, so the opportunity was lost. I was not in least bit bothered, because what I had been given the chance to experience was way more valuable.

The last workshop was the end of the tour and we were on the way back to Sarang and Lata's house. I was exhausted, but I was buzzing. I seriously thought about asking if I could stay for a few more days, just to get to experience more and find more about the *Shanti Project*. But I knew I had to keep on the move.

Sarang seemed to have really enjoyed my company and we could both see that we had a lot in common. I felt so lucky to have met him and Lata and I hoped we could remain in touch. Sarang was keen for us to work together and raise money from different sides of the planet. He suggested that as I would have walked the whole length of the Godavari River, I could promote interest and advertisement that would generate help for a new project he had in mind. He questioned whether I had noticed that the banks of the river were bare and eroding fast. I agreed, wondering where this conversation was going. He said he would like to run a huge scale project to protect the great river by planting bamboo all along the Godavari's river banks.

He said this project would (1) protect the river, (2) produce a product for India to sell and (3) provide work for a great number of the local population. I was more than interested as he talked and was impressed that he knew the river was more than 1200 kilometres long, so that would be a lot of bamboo trees to plant. As he talked, he mentioned that as Lata had given land to Shanti to start her project, maybe she would have some capital to start this project off. At this stage, I knew it was just an idea but here in India, anything is possible.

We returned to the house and I talked to their son, Loukric, who showed me how to do the Rubix Cube in less than one minute! I had a go and thought back to the 1980s, when I only ever managed to do that once and that was down to pure luck. In the evening, LB turned up with his two sons and we all had dinner together. He brought me flowers. Later that evening, we went out walking altogether. I bought some peanuts and dried fruits to give me energy for walking. We talked late into the night and I felt sure I would know these people forever. A week after writing this, they travelled to Mumbai on business and met up with my family.

Again, you would be hard pushed to make all this stuff up.

Sarang and Lata

Chapter 18
Sharad

With yesterday being so full on, I was just hoping that I could tick along alone, completely by myself today and reach my next stop.

After staying up till the small hours talking to Sarang, I had only had four and half hours' sleep, so I was bit worried about my energy levels when I started walking. Sarang had agreed to take me in his car to within walking distance of the next town, Purna, which was over forty kilometres from Parbhani. The plan was to drop me on the road about twenty one kilometres from Purna, where I hoped I could find a hotel. I said goodbye to Lata and Loukric (the Rubix Cube expert); LB had also arrived to say goodbye, so the three of us got into Sarang's car and hit the road. It wasn't long before we had reached the part where I was to be left on my own. But not before a goodbye cup of chai.

What wonderful people they were, and how lucky was I to have met them?

I said my goodbyes and took a side road towards Purna, my next place to sleep. The road was dusty, but it seemed pleasant enough; there was not much traffic, so I had no worries about being flatted by any trucks. It seemed only local vehicles used this road, so time moved on and I must have walked for over an hour without seeing a living soul.

Approaching a larger settlement, I hoped that this could be a place where I could get some more water. I had now been walking for four kilometres, so a water stop was needed soon. A young man approached me on his motor bike, asking if I was ok and if I needed a lift. I refused and continued on walking, but this man was very persistent and would ride off and then ten minutes later, he would return, asking the same questions. But somehow this man seemed different from all the others I had refused a lift from. He spoke good English and generally appeared concerned for my well-being. I smiled at him, but reassured him that I was ok and that I needed to walk. Understanding that I was walking for charity, he still wanted to help in any way that he could. I thanked him again for offering, but declined for the third time.

Finally, I found somewhere that I could drink water and when I stopped, the man and his bike was there waiting. I did find this a bit odd and started to worry that perhaps he was stalking me, but for whatever reason, I couldn't imagine this to be true.

We spoke some more, then I left the little water shack and was on my way again. The man left on his bike. After another ten minutes, I saw him again. This time he was sitting on his bike and waiting for me to pass. I had explained that I was walking to Purna earlier and this was where he wanted to give me a lift to. He then shouted from the other side of the road, '*Sir you have no need to walk to Purna to find a hotel, you can stay with me in my house*'. I didn't quite know what to say. I looked over the road at this young man, sitting on his bike, pointing to a house that was situated just off the main road. I smiled and continued to walk on, but he was so insistent to help, I stopped and thought for a moment. Maybe staying in this man's house could be better than staying in another dodgy hotel room. I trusted my instincts that this stranger who was offering to put me up for the night was ok and had no ulterior motive. I did, however, wonder how such a young man could own such a large house in rural India, situated in the middle of nowhere. I asked him where his parents were and he explained that he lived in the house, just himself and his grandmother. I felt the whole situation was a bit odd.

Having taken the time to stop, I could tell that this young man was certainly genuine and just wanted to help me if he could. I had only walked about six kilometres and it was another fifteen kilometres to my next stop. I looked at him and then the house and explained that I needed to carry on walking.

I explained that if I didn't walk every day for the whole morning or I didn't cover fifteen to twenty kilometres a day, I felt as though I had cheated myself.

I knew this man was determined to help so I made a really unusual suggestion; he was all ears. I suggested that I would continue to walk all the way to the next town in Purna. Once there, I would phone him and he could pick me up on his bike and bring me back to his house, where I would sleep. I saw by his face he was slightly puzzled, but he agreed nevertheless. The madness of the situation was for me to walk past his house then later, after walking fifteen kilometres, I would be driven back to the same house to sleep in. We exchanged phone numbers and I left, knowing that I would be seeing this man later. His name was Sharad, he was twenty-one and a good-looking young man. He was well-groomed and suited the baggy style clothing he was wearing. What was most striking about his appearance were his immaculate white teeth; they would not have been out of place in the mouth of an Indian Bollywood star. This strange decision to sleep in Sharad's house turned out to be one I will never forget.

I really didn't think that this day would, in any way, match up to the experience I had the day before, meeting Sarang, Lata and LB, but at the time, what did I know? Even though I was tired from the lack of sleep, having spoken with Sarang for most of the night, I was excited again. What had I agreed to?

A young man picking me up on a bike and driving me back to his big house in the middle of nowhere. I thought maybe the heat was now affecting my decision process.

When I finally arrived in Purna, I was not at all surprised by the dirt and mess the town offered its visitors. I was getting used to seeing rubbish lining the streets and smelling all sorts of unpleasant smells. I was completely blind to the poverty I was witnessing on a daily basis and that was sad. I didn't want to be blind to this and I had to reawaken myself every time I saw such scenes. Making it easily into the town centre, I needed to redress my feet quickly and drink as much water as I possibly could. I found a shack opposite the railway station, thinking that if I was going to phone Sharad, this would be an easy place for him to find me. Sitting down, drinking water and mending my feet, I soon had the usual crowd around me. Once again, I produced the golden ticket and all sorts of locals were shaking my hand. I spoke to some civil engineers who worked on the trains; we had a conversation about how old the cabins on the trains were and what condition they were in.

They said that most of the train cabins here were mobile and of British design. They were built in the 1960s. They said that they were old but really well built and built to last, the good old British. Yes, once we were so good.

I phoned Sharad and true to his word, there he was on his bike. However, he was not on his own when he arrived. I was surprised to see him with a friend.

To make it more surprising, he and his friend both had a bike. I was told to go on the back of his friend's bike, so again I found myself, rucksack and all, on the back of a stranger's bike, but a stranger that I had never seen or spoke to before in my life. Sharad explained that this other man was his cousin, Sachin, who was a safer and more experienced rider; I was to travel with him. Who was I to argue? I climbed on the bike and tried to make conversation this man who just nodded and said nothing. Sharad explained that Sachin spoke no English. I nodded, patted him on the back and off we went. He, like Sharad, became an instant friend.

I arrived back at Sharad's house to lunch and chai was prepared by his grandmother. He explained that his father had died last year and both his sister and mother had had to go to the large city to work. He was left in charge of the farm, the house and the responsibility of looking after his grandmother. All this and he was only just twenty-one.
He had had to mature early, and after speaking to him for a while, he appeared a lot older than his years suggested. I sat on the floor with him and his cousin in the lounge, eating the lunch provided.
 I knew I had made the right decision in accepting Sharad's invitation to stay the night.

But it wasn't long before Sharad had spread the word that there was a stranger in town, and a white stranger at that, which made it all the more exciting. Within minutes of my arrival, I was surrounded by a group of men, mainly young teenagers. Everyone was introduced as they entered Sharad's lounge. All smiling and wanting to talk to me. I was overwhelmed yet again. I felt very awkward and had not been in such young company since I was young. Soon there were about fifteen adolescent men all staring at me, watching me eat my lunch. Some were lucky enough to be sitting on the one sofa in the lounge; the others just sat next to me on the floor.

Sharad was obviously in charge and he ordered one of the younger teenagers to go out on his bike and bring back a huge container of fresh drinking water, complete with its own tap. It seemed that all the young men sort of looked up to Sharad; there was something about him that just said *trust me and follow me.*

I was one of those people. Then he told me something about his village that to a westerner, seemed beyond belief.

The village, with over three thousand people, was called Katneshwar. Sharad explained that it only had power for twelve hours a day as people in the village could not afford to pay for more than that. He said it was an unfair situation where some people were paying for power and others were not, mainly because they couldn't afford it. The solution was solved when the power company decided if they did not get all the money required, they would only supply the power for twelve hours, and that was to everyone, regardless if you paid or not. I wasn't really sure how I felt about that decision, but he continued to talk and I continued to listen. He then revealed the most shocking piece of information: *Do you realise that you are the first white person ever to walk through this village and you are certainly the first white person to ever stay here?* At first, I didn't believe him, but as more and more men from the village turned up to meet me, I started to think that this could be true. I was nowhere near a town, or a proper road and nowhere near any tourist attraction so why would a white person (or any foreigner for that matter) come to a place like this? Was there any need for a white person to be here? However, I was different. I was on a mission following the Godavari and this village, just by luck, was on my route.

I thought back to some of those travel programs I had watched, where someone had been flown into the rainforest and had stumbled upon a lost tribe that had never seen anyone from the outside world. Did this situation really have anything in common with that? Was my walk across India making history here right in front of my eyes? Was I making history? Wow, I thought.

During the next few hours, more and more of the villagers and Sharad's friends made the effort to come to see me. Sharad enjoyed the attention and was acting like a bouncer at a nightclub on the door of his house, deciding who he felt had a right to meet the white star. Then one man entered the lounge, a slightly older man. I would have perhaps aged him about mid to late twenties. He seemed to have more importance than Sharad. We were introduced and he sat on the only chair, opposite the sofa. He then just fired off as many questions as he could, about why I was here and what my purpose was. He was the only person in the whole village that had been fully educated at university.

Sharad later explained that he himself had started university, but had had to stop when his father died. It seemed that this man sitting on the chair was the real brains of the village and was sent to make sure that my intentions were good

He even asked to see my identification, noticing that my Indian visa would run out at the end of May. At times he appeared rude, but answering all his questions the best I could, I understood that he was only looking after the people of the village. After some ten minutes, the interrogation was over and we all relaxed. Sharad decided to make the whole situation a little less serious and said he would put some music on. He used his oversized stereo that filled nearly an entire corner of the room. I sat back and thought what a strange situation to be in, but I relaxed and was ready to enjoy some Bollywood style music, but I was surprised. It was not Bollywood; it was Johnny Cash. I smiled at Sharad, and he said *just for you sir*. How could this lovely man that I had just met possibly have known that I liked Johnny Cash. Not only did I like Johnny Cash, but Johnny Cash's music featured quite heavily at my wedding. When the music stopped, the serious man got up from the chair, shook my hand and said perhaps I might see him later at their temple. I nodded and agreed. He then confirmed what Sharad had said earlier; I was the only white person to ever pass by and visit their village. After Sharad's friends had recovered from their excitement of meeting a white man, Sharad asked if I would be interested in looking at their farm.

Of course, I agreed and soon there were three motor bikes waiting outside Sharad's house. Now there were only six of us that drove out to the farm and I was put with Sharad's cousin, Sachin, again. Sharad said that both he and his cousin owned ten acres each and worked the land together. We rode off and soon reached some distant fields. I felt so lucky to be seeing this. We were deep in rural India and I was excited to learn how these new friends of mine survived. Sharad was keen to share his knowledge and was extremely proud of his farm and so he should have been. He said that during the summer, most of the fields produced sugar cane, (that reminded me of Prakash's farm), but he said they also produced some mangos and chillies. In the rainy season, the fields were used to grow soya beans. All six of us walked around the fields, looking at the drainage and the water pumps that were used to pump water from the ground to water the crops. Sharad explained that you had to dig three hundred and fifty feet down into the hard, hot earth to find water and one of the men that was with us, Ram Chapke, tried to explain that this was his father's job. Sharad explained that this man's father had the skill to know where on the fields to look and how far down had to drill to get water. I was amazed. We walked further into the field, took photographs under a mango tree and even tasted one, but it was not ripe. All the time, my bike rider friend Sachin was by my side smiling and Sharad translated what he wanted to say to me. We stopped at a shepherd's hut, where red onions were all over the floor and took more photographs of each other.

There was manual oxen machinery that we pulled over our heads and took more photographs. To me, the machinery looked like it should have come from a museum in the Industrial Revolution, but this was their equipment that they were still using. There were fields in every direction; no engines or modern technology in sight. All the work was still done by man and beast, the ox. I lay on a wooden bed and rested. Sharad told me that they came to sleep here for many nights especially when they were working the land. He told me how they needed to work when there was light. To plough one field with the ox can take a whole week and that is working from sun up until sun down. But he then said we have to take our chances when we sleep out here with the stars as we are at risk of being bitten by a snake. I nodded and try to explain to him that was why I had decided to get rid of my tent. I then met Sachin's father and he let me pat one of the working oxen. He, like his son, had a real calmness about him. It is hard to explain in words, but he was just a man that was happy with life and happy with what he was fortunate enough to own. He did not seem to want anything else from life, except peace and calm.

We left the farm and, on a convoy of motor bikes, returned to the village, but not to Sharad's house.

His house was too small for all the additional interest my arrival had caused. It had been organised that we were to all meet at the school; a sad looking building that had been developed over the years, with the newest part dating from the 70's. Thinking about it, probably every person that I had met had gone to that school so, apart from the temples, it remained the hub of the community. I arrived on the back of Sachin's bike to cheers and claps; there were about forty more young men and boys all sitting in a circle on the school field waiting for my arrival. I had to sit down in the circle where everyone could get a proper view of their guest star. They were then all interested in seeing my passport, and it was passed around the circle. I then showed them my pen knife and that gained more interest; they were asking how much it would cost. I met a man in a wheel chair who, other than Sharad and the serious man I had met earlier, was the only person who had good enough English for a conversation.

Back to Sharad's house where his grandmother cooked me more food. It was evening and the crowds had disappeared; it was so good to be able to speak to Sharad on his own. He asked if I would like to visit a temple in the centre of the village. I agreed, so back on the bike; this time I was on his bike and just one other friend joined us.

We looked around the temple and just enjoyed the peace. Not many words were exchanged as we looked around, but I felt in awe, imagining that this temple, hundreds of years old and I was the only white western person to have ever visited it.

We left the temple, saying *goodnight* to Sharad's friend and returning to Sharad's house. It had been a long day and Sharad had agreed that he would give me a lift to the town where he had picked me up earlier, in order for my journey to continue. It had been such a busy, overwhelming day, that not once had I thought about where I would be sleep that night. So, when we returned to the house, I just assumed that Sharad would sleep in his room and I would take the sofa. But that was not the case. Sharad, (just like Prekash earlier in my trip), wanted to sleep in the same room as me.

It was a normal thing that Indian friends do, and I had become a friend so quickly, that I was honoured to be sharing a room. A mattress was produced from nowhere and we soon lay together on the lounge floor. The portable AC unit was off and the windows were opened. We needed torch light to sort out the pillows and sheets as all the power was off in the whole village. The torch light provided an instant attraction for all sorts of flying insects and soon it seemed that my mattress was walking with creatures. Sharad assured me that once the torches were turned off, the creatures would disappear. I wasn't convinced, but I laid down in the darkness and tried not to think too much about whom I was sharing my bed with.

Laying on the floor in the dark, despite my tiredness, it became apparent that it wasn't time to sleep yet. Sharad wanted to talk to me and I wanted to listen. This young man that I had only met earlier today had helped me, shown me around his farm, his temple, introduced me to nearly the whole village, fed me twice and given me somewhere to sleep. But during this whole time, we had hardly got the chance to speak, I just knew he was a great person and I was interested to hear his story. When he started to talk to me whilst we lay on the floor, the first thing that I found amazing was how mature he was for someone of twenty-one. Not having had much experience talking to young adults, I was sure the ones I had spoken to didn't act like this man. I suppose we all stereotype people into age groups, but I never dreamt that it would take a walk across India to make me realise we can learn from anyone, regardless of their age. It made me think: why I would assume that someone had to be of a certain age, before they could help me and, more importantly, that they had to be of a certain age before I could learn from them? In the dark, Sharad opened up and started talking about his father who had died only last year. He spoke like a man with great experience of life. He told me his father was a drunk, who had often beaten him when he was a child.

His family had tried to stop him drinking for as long as he could remember, but he wouldn't listen. He said his father had not died quickly; his liver just started to close down. But not before the continuous medical treatments had wiped out all the family's money. Operations and medical treatment had been paid for, for his father to get better, promising not to drink again. But as soon as he was out of hospital, he would hit the bottle again and again. Sharad explained this very sad situation, but with no anger or remorse. He had accepted what had happened, realising he could do nothing about it and was now trying to put right the situation that his father had left the family in. Now the man of the house, it was his job to provide for his family. His mother and two sisters were working away, trying to raise money by working in a factory. One his sisters was soon to be married, so it was his responsibility to find the funds for her arranged marriage. I laid still and listened.

He was worried that his ten-acre farm would not be able to produce the money he needed to support the family. He asked what crops I thought he should plant in his fields. I looked at the ceiling. I knew there must have been a reason for doing a geography degree; was this it?

But I had no answers. He talked about replacing the sugar cane with tomatoes, but knew that the life time for the tomatoes was not long enough.

If you cannot sell the tomatoes when they become ripe, then they would be worthless. I agreed. I had seen items in the Indian news where farmers were so upset at being unable to sell their produce, that they had thrown thousands of tomatoes into the road, turning the tarmac red. He asked my advice on all sorts of things and I was really struggling to point this unfortunate young farmer in the right direction. Did I think that a chicken farm would bring more profits, or chillies? We spoke and I comforted him, trying to assure him that he would make the right decision, but as far as my farming advice went, I would say it was pretty worthless.

Finally, we must have just drifted off to sleep. But not for long, as at 3.00am there was a knock on the door and Sachin, with a few friends, entered the lounge where we were sleeping. I wondered what was going on. Sharad reassured me they had been working and always crashed here at this time rather than waking their families up. He explained briefly while I was trying to open my eyes that they had been working on the farm. At this time, I thought, but he then went onto to say that they had been working with the turmeric. They were boiling the roots, which later they used to make turmeric powder. They did this at such an hour, to allow them to work on the farm during the daylight hours and boil the turmeric when the day's temperature was at its lowest. I felt amazed that all these experiences were happening around me.

Breakfast was served about two hours later and we waited for first light, so I could get back on the Sachin's bike to be dropped off at the local railway station. I had planned a route; Nanded was my next available town with accommodation and it was too far to get to without transport. I was going to jump the train and get off at a place called Wanegaon and walk from there. Soon I was back on the bike with Sachin driving and Sharad and Ram Chapke riding alongside me on their bikes. It was about sixteen kilometres to the railway station and the place I had already reached the day before. It felt so good to be out so early in the morning, watching all the people going about their daily routines, but for a change I wasn't walking past them, I was riding past them. People in the village had made a special effort to get up early and wave their goodbyes. The wind was in my hair and I had never felt so alive as I did at that moment. Then without warning, I started to cry, I didn't know where it had come from, but I was completely overwhelmed by this occasion. Sharad saw me crying as he drove next to me, saying *sir, please don't cry you should be happy that you have met some new friends.* I think I was crying because these people had made such an impression on me. I patted Sachin on the shoulder in the same way I had the first time I had met him and, just like me, he shed a tear. I thought how this could be possible to make such a close bond with someone that who did not share my language and that I had only known for less than twenty four hours? If someone had explained that something like this could happen before I started this trip, I would never have believed them.

At the railway station, the bikes were parked. I went to say goodbye but they were not finished with me yet, and I, along with these three young men, all walked to the railway station, Sharad carrying my rucksack. He then said he would get my ticket and refused to take any money for it. By now I knew it was pointless trying to argue with him; I was his guest and he was going to pay.

We waited for the train on the platform, all feeling a bit emotional and I was still trying to hold the tears back. Sharad approached another man and asked what train I needed to catch, asking this man who, luckily, was going the same way, to look after me. He explained my mission and the man agreed he would help me off of the train when it reached Wanegaon. Soon the train arrived and sitting next to the window after saying goodbye, the three men appeared, this time to pass through packets of biscuits that they had just bought in the station. I thanked them, shook their hands and the train started to move.

Yet more friends I think I will know forever.

Sharad and Sachin

Chapter 19
Wanegaon and Wagi

Rural India flitted past outside the train window. I leant back and enjoyed the moment. It was a proper rural train and just as basic as those I was used to travelling on in Mumbai. I knew that before too long, I would be walking a full day to get to Nanded so I wanted to appreciate this rare time of rest. The man that Sharad had asked to look after me informed me that this was my stop. Trains do not stop long at these isolated stations so I knew I did not have much time to disembark. It was a steep descent; I needed more help from the man, who held my rucksack as I got down. With the train moving off, the man threw me my rucksack. Wanegaon station reminded me of a dusty, old town, something that you might expect to see in a Clint Eastwood film. There was nothing to see except railway track and dust. The train disappeared along the track and I just stood there thinking, this time, I really am alone. I consulted Google maps and asked the odd person what way I needed to go to reach another small village called Wagi. I had planned a route that would give me a chance to drink water before reaching the big city of Nanded. Leaving the railway track, I followed a dust path.

I had real no idea if I was even walking in the correct direction. I thought about my wife Michelle and how we used to go for walks back in the UK. She always had to know exactly how far the walk was, every point of interest we were passing and how long (approximately) the walk would take. I was, and still am, the total opposite. For me, not knowing where I am going makes it exciting. I thought that at this precise moment in time, she would have hated this, walking on a dust track, not knowing where it was going or even if it was heading in the correct direction. For the first time on the trip, my compass was used and I was happy just strolling along. I bumped into two ladies who, in view of the path, were performing their early morning ablutions. I scared them and they ran further into the wilds to save any more embarrassment. I thought they must have been doing the same act every morning for years and, that particular morning, a white man with a pink hat appeared. I wondered what they thought and, after seeing me, would they return to their toileting grounds tomorrow?

I continued down the path, soon passing a small farm. The farmer and his son were really surprised to see me and invited me to sit down with them, just outside a cow shed. We had the same familiar communication problems, but all the smiles just seemed to make any frustration disappear. There was also a very annoying small dog that seemed obligatory in most farms in India.

But after I had been sitting for a while, communicating with its owners, it calmed down and even let me stroke it. I had to move on, having eighteen kilometres of walking ahead of me, so sitting down in the early morning sun on yet another rural Indian farm, as good as it was, was not going to help me reach my final destination. However, I couldn't help but notice the activities in the cow shed. I had arrived just after a cow had just given birth and the mother was eating the after-birth. I had been lucky enough to witness this once before on the Downs, but that was years ago and somehow, I felt, was nowhere near as memorable. But not to the farmer and his son who looked surprised when I stopped to take photographs. I explained that I need to move on and the farmer signalled to his son to lead me on the dusty path to get me back to civilisation. As I walked along the path with the farmer's son, I was joined by two more small children, the boy's friends; they could not have been any older than seven years of age and just seemed to appear from nowhere. I was pleased with the company and we walked along the path for nearly one hour. Then they stopped walking and pointed for me to continue; they shook my hand and returned to walk back to their farms. I needed water and soon, I arrived at the small village on my route called Wagi. I asked several people where I could buy water. They were more than surprised to see me walking alone, but pointed me in the right direction.

I was expecting the usual shop-cum-shack on the side of the road, the type of place I had been buying water from on this walk, but there seemed to be no shops in sight. Was everyone in this village totally self-sufficient I thought? Walking on, I found myself outside what looked like a car garage, and a man appeared when I asked for water. He then happily filled my water bottle from a large container and would take no money. He then phoned his friend who, in less than two minutes, arrived on a motor bike and wanted to drive me to Nanded. I refused, explaining that I needed to walk. He smiled and pointed me on the long road ahead to Nanded. As I walked out of town, there was a large gathering of people and a band of people playing all sorts of instruments, including trumpets. I wanted to stay and join in the fun of this local festival, but the walking forced me on. As I passed, I think I might have even allowed myself a little hip sway in time with the beat.

Before this walk and even more so since I started walking, I had never really been a dog lover; I have always preferred cats. Every morning before the sun rises, I am greeted by barks and mini attacks, so my love for man's four-legged friend has not improved. Hiking along another long straight road, I was soon approached by a small dog, a pup and it seemed to be really friendly. I am always cautious about befriending dogs and I have always taken the approach if they want to know me, they will; if they don't, I am not bothered.

Being a runner back in the UK, I am often stopped by barking dogs, most of the time they are just trying to be friendly; nevertheless I have always considered them as a pain. But today after stroking the farmer's dog earlier and being approached by Pup, maybe my view would change.

This dog just would not let me out of its sight and we walked along the road for over an hour together. I spoke to it, stroked it and being soft-hearted, I even gave it some of the biscuits that I eat whilst walking. It was my friend and companion. But after another half an hour it decided that it would stop walking with me and turned the way it had just came and disappeared.

You always know when you are moving from rural roads to coming close to a town. It's obvious, but the amount of traffic increases. This, in a strange way, gives you hope and you realise that you haven't got too much further to go before you can rest for the evening.

Approaching Nanded, the roads became busier and busier and this place seemed much like many of the other towns I had walked through; just another dirty, old town - I am sure there is a song in there somewhere. But these dirty old towns gave me something I need - unless I am lucky enough to meet someone - they gave me somewhere to sleep.

Sarang had arranged for one of his friends to meet me. This friend had phoned me and told me that he would meet me at the Bus Station in Nanded, so that was where I was heading. Yet again, it had been another full day's walking and I needed to stop soon. The usual enemies were appearing: blisters, exhaustion and the sun. I reached the Station and Sarang phoned me, confirming his young friend was on his way. I found a shack, drank some water and rested my feet. I imagined some man would arrive to pick me up, show me the sites, feed me and let me stay in his house. I had been so lucky over the last few days that I just expected this luck to continue. Eventually, two men turned up on motor bikes and introduced themselves as friends of Sarang. I found myself on the back of one of the bikes riding through Nanded not knowing what to expect or having any idea where I was going. I trusted Sarang though, so I knew I would be safe.

Soon my driver arrived at a social office in Nanded. I knew Sarang was a social worker, so he was using his contacts to make sure I was safe. In rapid Hindi, the rider explained my mission to two men in the office, shook my hand and left. I found a chair and leant back, just happy to be feeling some AC on my skin. I knew I had to air my feet, so I peeled off my socks and shoes and tended to my most important asset.

The two men in the office attempted to talk to me in broken English. I explained my mission to both of them and was met with utter silence. No one in this office really knew why I was there, me included and, more importantly, none of them knew what I wanted, or what they were supposed to do to help me. I had just been dropped on them and it felt a bit awkward. Fate was on my side and one of the social workers, Vijay decided he would take the lead. He said he would find me a budget hotel where I could sleep for the night. After more water, I was soon on another bike riding around town, with Vijay trying to find somewhere I could sleep. But that wasn't easy as we tried two hotels and both were fully booked. Fortunately, Vijay wasn't just going to let me fend for myself and he just kept driving around until a hotel was found.

I was so grateful for Vijay's help and I thanked him with all my heart. I was so tired after a full day's walking and then having to find the energy to talk and thank all these kind people I was meeting was really taking its toll. I said goodbye after Vijay had found me a room and negotiated a price for the night. The hotel was very basic, but I knew that I probably wouldn't even have the energy to eat, so as long as it had a bed and a lock on the door, I would be happy.

Entering the room, I saw one of the biggest cockroaches I have ever seen in my life in the bathroom, but I was too tired and just shut the door.

All I need was a bucket from the bathroom, and I would have no need to go back in there again.

I looked out of my bedroom window and saw that my room was situated above a small rubbish dump; that was nothing unusual. But as I looked closely, I saw pigs, cows, dogs, goats, monkeys and rats all living happily together, trying to find food.
Taking my shoes off for the fourth time that day, I noticed another problem... I was missing the big toe nail on my left foot.

My young guides

Chapter 20
Broccoli or Slop

I couldn't believe it was the weekend again. The time had gone so fast; now I would get to chat to my sons and speak about the English Premium league scores. Was the time going so fast because I was enjoying myself?

The days seemed to take two parts: the first part, the daily physically, mind-blowing morning of walking; the second part, meeting people that would allow me into their lives.

Studying the map yesterday and speaking to various people, I knew that, once again, I was faced with the same problem of nowhere to stay. None of the small villages that I had planned to walk through had any accommodation. After waking at 4.30am this morning, I knew I would have to take a bus in order to reach somewhere I could start walking from to allow me to reach accommodation safely in one full day's walking. Jumping off the bus in a place called Kahala, I walked through an industrial town called Krishnur. I assumed, because of its size, there would be accommodation but when I started to walk through it, I realised that there was no place to stay, there was no accommodation.

There were huge buildings along the side of the road, belching out smoke fumes into the once pure, rural Indian air. I looked up at the fumes as I strolled passed and the only thought that came into my mind was that this pollution was all down to us, the human race.

Walking cautiously along a fast-main road, I tried to not think about the dangerous traffic all around me. Something large crossed the road in front of me; a monkey, a black-faced monkey, fortunately not the same breed of monkey that attacked me on the first day of my walk. It seemed to be playing with the traffic, like a school child would play *English Bull Dog*, using all its tag skills of dodging, increasing and decreasing its pace as to avoid the fast passing traffic. Normally something like this would have been a wow moment for me, but I just looked, smiled to myself and just carried on walking.

This day passed without too much more excitement and I soon found a hotel on the outside of the town, with no AC, no English, nowhere to eat, but a bed. I ventured out to try to find somewhere to eat; it was just after mid-day and I couldn't find anywhere open. The heat was approaching 50°C, so I knew walking around lost and hungry was not a sensible option.

I found somewhere to get water and it also sold samosas so this, teamed up with some cheap biscuits, was my evening meal. I was soon surrounded by locals all wanting to have a selfie and trying to understand why I was in their town. After eating the samosas and biscuits, I needed to get out of the heat. I returned to my hotel room. My whole day was over by 1.00pm. I washed, completed my blog and waited for the day to pass so I could continue walking again tomorrow.

The next morning started in the same vein as every morning: mending my feet and getting my rucksack ready for a full day of walking. My next stop was a place called Bololi, and every time I looked at the name on the map, it reminded me of *broccoli*. This took me back to cooking and eating Sunday roast, all safe and cosy in my house back in Framlingham, Suffolk. I often day dreamed and simple things like a word, sight or smell would transport me back to a place I had good safe memories of.

Then the day dream would break and I would be back walking, with blistered feet and numb shoulders, through the heat of the Indian sun beating down on me.

I walked through places called Narisi and Kasrasihi, where I was stopped for more selfies and conversation with groups of thirty men all trying to understand my mission - not one woman in sight.

Clothing in India differs greatly from the city to the countryside. A *Lunghi* is a garment worn by Indian men. The simplest way to describe it, from a western point of view, without meaning to offend, would be say it looks like an expansive towel wrapped around a man's waist and folded up in between the man's groin. I have spoken to many men and they all say it is very comfortable and lets the air flow around those specific, regions that require air flow in the Indian heat. It is worn as relaxed ware and Ghandi was famous for always wearing one, but to me it looked far from comfortable or relaxed.

As I was walking, a man wearing a *lunghi* approached me and, in Hindi, spoke to me. I think he asked if he could join me in walking.

I produced my golden ticket. He then kissed his hands and touched my feet. This had happened to me before whilst I was walking and some young pupils (that I had taught in the slum school) also performed this act. It was the utmost respect that you could give someone. I was embarrassed, but humbled by this man's gesture. He then mumbled on in Hindi and I could only guess that he wanted me to follow him, so I did. He crossed the busy road that I had been walking on for some time, and walked me up to the front of a huge house. I looked up at it and it looked like a palace. It also looked really out of place, standing there, on its own, by the side of a road in the middle of rural India.

Welcomed in by the whole family and, with hardly any English being spoken, I was shown up a flight of steep outdoor marble stairs. These opened up into a vast marbled open-air space, filled with all sorts of decorated seats. All of this was outside of the main house and I was soon ushered into a seat. The man wearing the *lungi*, explained my mission to the eagerly listening family. Like lots of families in India, there were three generations all living under one roof. The young children were shy at first, but soon started to smile and accepted me as an unexpected guess in their house. The mother and grandmother soon went to work and before I had time to take my shoes and socks off, chapattis and drinks were being served.

It was then time for the men of the house to talk to me. I explained that I needed to treat my feet and all the family were fascinated and all watched the changing of the plasters. First a younger man tried to talk to me (I would guess he was younger than twenty and his English was the best of the family). He lifted my rucksack and the weight knocked him off balance and he just managed to stop himself from falling over - everyone laughed. I think he was really impressed that I was carrying such a weight all across India. An older man appeared, full of smiles and appeared to be happy that I had visited their house. He explained that he used to be in the Indian army.

He showed me a photo on his phone to prove the fact. He then lifted my rucksack with one hand placed it on his back, as if to say 'no problem I am ex-army'. The older man in the *lunghi* left and I thanked him for introducing me to this family. The ex-army man explained, with the help of the younger man, that he had just married the younger's man's sister and that the wedding had taken place here at the house two days previously. The wife then appeared and again, it was all smiles, as I was shown around the outside of the house, looking at all the decorations that were still remaining from the wedding. It reminded me of a film that I had watched some years ago with Michelle called *Monsoon Wedding*. I wished I had arrived in time to share in their wedding celebrations.

I then had to make a decision: should I continue to talk and hope that these people would continue their generosity and let me sleep the night. Or, should I part company now, with time allowing me to be able to reach the next town before the temperatures became unbearable. I decided that, as lovely has these people were, I needed to keep moving. I thanked them for the food, drink and their warm welcomes, but explained that I needed to continue walking. They understood and we smiled, nodded and parted. However just as I was going to walk down the marble staircase, the younger man that had struggled to lift my rucksack stopped me at the top of the stairs and said that I was the first and only western that had ever entered their house.

I had seven kilometres left to walk into the next town and find my next accommodation and, because I hadn't overstayed my welcome at the house of marble, I felt that this would be easily achievable. Walking along, I could feel the sun approaching its mid-day heat, so I increased my pace to get out of the heat as soon as possible.

I was approached by another young man on a motor bike - nothing unusual, in fact, as you know, something that I was very used to dealing with. A friendly man, whose English was good; he wanted a selfie, which I obliged and he also wanted to give me a lift. I explained that I was walking, produced my golden ticket, the message he totally understood and soon left me to continue my stroll into town. After another thirty minutes, I saw the same young man on his bike at a petrol garage. I waved and he approached me again. I had less than two kilometres to the town so I felt I had time to talk. He was really persistent that I should jump on his bike and he would drive me into town. I don't know why I agreed to take him up on his offer this time, but again, it proved to be the best decision I could have made. Once more my walk across India had found a way of putting me on a stranger's motor bike. We chatted as he drove on. His name was Munna Lanke and he was another person I will never forget.

He drove us to a small shack on the side of the road and indicated *'canna'* - food. He ordered dosas that were made by several men using their hands in a way I had never witnessed before.

The dough was rolled between their two fists before it was paced on a large hot plate to cook. Munna spoke to me, but I was fascinated by the way these dosas were being made. He ordered water and then paid for the food. It was the best food I had eaten since I had started this adventure. I tried to pay my way, but Munna would not let me. He explained that he was a secretary or has he described it 'I am a typer.' He explained that he still used the old-fashioned typewriters, but the other month his employer got their first computer! We exchanged numbers and he agreed that he would take me to my lodgings, which was really just over the other side of the road. Approaching the hotel, there didn't seem to be any sign of life. It looked totally closed. Munna held his hands up in the air as if you say, 'I didn't know that the only hotel in town was closed'. He walked next door and spoke to a man in a small store, then returned to me, where I was still waiting on the back of his motor bike. He explained that the hotel had been closed for over a year and went on to explain that there was no need for hotels, as people just didn't stay there. This was an industrial town and it only survived due to the large sugar cane factories, (the ones that I had walked past earlier).

There were no tourists and no one needed to sleep or stay here other than the people that lived here. It was very unusual for any foreigners to be seen around here in this town and that explained why I was the first and only westerner to visit that house earlier. But all this information really didn't help me; after walking for nearly six hours, I had nowhere to sleep. Munna explained that the only option was to get to the next town. He explained that it was bigger and would certainly have accommodation there. He also explained that, due to the distance, it would not be advisable for me to walk there. I was also thinking the same thing. I had already walked all day, and the sun was now at it hottest. For me to walk another six hours would be a certain way to end this trip and not the way I had planned.

Munna said that he would drop me off at the bus station and I would have to catch a bus to the next town, Bodhan, so the idea of sleeping in a town that reminded me of broccoli had vanished. We soon arrived at the bus station and, parking his bike, Munna ran into the station at such a pace that I was left struggling to get off of his bike on my own. He knew the buses and knew that the one that I needed to catch. The problem was that it was just about to leave! He managed to stop the bus before it left the station and the bus grudgingly waited for me to get on. I climbed aboard, absolutely exhausted and fell into a seat with my rucksack on my lap.

I had no idea where I was going and no energy to do anything about it. The bus left the station, but then as I looked out of the window, I saw Munna following the bus, and I thought to myself, what I have forgotten? He then drove alongside the bus as it was moving and started shouting, in a nice way so that he could be heard over the noise of bus's engine. He drove alongside, having a conversation with the bus driver, telling him that he must look after me. And that I need a hotel to sleep in in Bodhan. The bus driver agreed to what Munna was saying, looked at me, nodded and smiled. I meet Munna's eyes once more through the window of the bus, and I thanked him again. Munna smiled at me, then pulled his bike back and he was gone. I sat and smiled at the bus driver, who smiled back. I was, yet again, amazed how many different people were helping me through my mission. Faith again, I hear myself say. Faith.

When the bus eventually stopped in Bodhan, all the people got off the bus. The bus driver parked the bus then personally walked me to the hotel, where he explained to the owner to give me the best room for the cheapest price. I said goodbye to yet another helpful person and checked in.

I needed to eat and, after dumping my rucksack, I ventured out into the town. Depending on how I am feeling, I have sort of got a strange routine going on: after I have found somewhere to sleep, I eat, then bed. However, even finding somewhere to eat can have its own sort of problems. I have found that the more rural my walk, the less chance of me ever being understood. There is no English anywhere and to find any person who can understand me with my broken Hindi is becoming less and less frequent. I was now in Telangana State where the language spoken was Telagu. I was passing through Indian states where even Hindi was not spoken. The man from the hotel suggested that if I wanted to eat then I should go to another hotel, with a restaurant, around the corner from where I am staying called *Kwality Hotel Bodhan*. I soon found it and after such a full day, I didn't think anything memorable could possibly happen to me before this day was over. But how wrong could I be. The heat was approaching 45°C and I could feel a dryness in my mouth. I didn't only need to eat, I also needed water. I walked into this eating establishment and I can only say it reminded me of the hospital I had visited last week with Sarang. But the further I moved into the building, to think that this reminded me of a hospital would be too kind a way to describe this place. It really was more like a prison. There was a totally washed out green colour on the walls and to use this colour even in a public outside toilet would be a bad decision. Tables were cramped into any space that was available, but mostly lined in rows against the green walls.

I just stood there looking, expecting a prison guard to pop out of the kitchen, grab me by throat and throw me into a cell. Standing, I felt like I had been there for an age, the length of a prison sentence. I looked and looked but had no real grasp of what was happening. I looked at the tables and I could see all the prisoners eating, but I had no idea how I could join them. Metal plates were being thrown in every direction and food, that could only be described as slop, was finding its way onto the plates before it entered the diners' mouths. I had time to turn around and walk away, calling this a bad idea, but something stopped me and I remained, watching. Eventually I saw a space became available on one of the tables and, without wanting to, my feet lead me to a metal chair and I sat down. I was still in a daze and then I realised that if I wanted to eat, I would have to communicate in some way. Menus were non-existent. There were none on the walls, like you might see in a gastro pub; none of the normal paper versions on the tables. Even if I had understood Telagu, to order would be impossible. To say that I felt like a foreigner completely lost would only be the start of how I felt. I had been lucky enough to do lots of travelling over the years and had found myself in many different countries and put myself in very unusual situations. But this was very different. I was so out of place that the locals didn't even notice me sitting there. It seemed beyond the unusual. Where so far on the trip, people were usually amazed and even shocked by my presence, here there was nothing. No one even gave me a second look or wondered why I was sitting there, trying to get some food. It simply felt that I didn't exist, an alien in New York, so yes I was, except this was far from being New York or anything close to it in any way imaginable. Sometimes I have felt that I was so different it was almost like being in a zoo, where everyone just looked at you and stared. Here this white monkey interested no one. I sat and thought the only way I am going to get fed is to copy what all these other prisoners were doing. I thought there must be some sort of system for all the people to follow. All I needed to do was sit, observe and then copy. First stop, where was this food slop coming from? The kitchen, where it was being cooked, would be the obvious answer and I scanned the dark green room to see if I could locate that. Yes, it was in the corner and five or six men were running in and out of this room, returning with the slop, or I should say, food. Pushing through the swing door, without any communication, they were missing each other and getting on with their business. This place was packed full and there were a lot of mouths to be fed. People say when you are travelling, first make sure that the place where you eat is busy and then you can be sure that the food will be good. This place was bursting at the seams; but the food looked far from good. Further observations made it clear that these men running in and out of the kitchen were, of course, the waiters.

All male, and as I looked around to see who was eating, this was obviously a male-only prison. I had identified the waiters, so all I had to do was to get their attention and order some food. Easy? Far from it! I sat there wondering if one of these runners would bother to come to me or would I have to leave my seat and approach them and somehow order food without any language. It was all a giant puzzle and I couldn't even start to put the pieces together, I only could find the four corners - all the rest was missing. I stayed sitting, watching, still wondering how I was ever going to get some food. I noticed that all the waiters that went into the kitchen soon came out and gathered around the centre of the room. Here, there was a large table, with four wide, large metal jugs. These were a combination of something between a jug and a bowl. Each one contained a ladle, and even though it was dark and I was a fair distance from the table, I could see dried up brown food hanging over the edges of these large vessels. Next to these jugs were huge plastic containers that held the water, (not too dissimilar to the one Sharad had used to keep me and his friends watered on his farm). On the floor next to the table, were two enormous dustbin look-a-likes: one was used for all the leftover food and the other was for all the dirty metal plates. These metal plates had four holes (or slots) on them that I could only imagine that was where the food would be served into. On the table, the clean metal plates were stacked so high they nearly reached the ceiling. This was large scale food distribution.

The closest I had seen before would be in a school, where the poor dinner ladies had to feed four hundred children in forty five minutes. Any way to save time and get things done quickly and efficiently is used. I wasn't too shocked when I noticed these dustbins; they were there to serve a purpose. The food needed to be dished out and dirty plates needed to be returned as quickly as possible. I was still sitting at the table, still wondering how and what to do next. I was now in a bit of a trance and I felt more comfortable just watching than I had done when I first came into this place. I looked around further and noticed there was not one knife, fork or spoon anywhere. This was a hands-only eating place. That wasn't new to me, but when I looked more closely at the consistency of the food, being of a liquid nature, if I did ever get served it could be an interesting experience to find a way to eat it. I decided that if I wanted to eat, then I would have to get up and approach one of the waiters. I was just about to leave my seat when three young men entered the room. They looked around and decided to sit next to me. Had I been saved from embarrassment? Could these men perhaps order for me? But as they sat down there was no acknowledgement that I was even sitting there. However, their presence, unlike mine, had caught the attention of one of the waiters and after they had only been sitting there for less than a minute, the waiter was over to the table. I did wonder why he had not come over to me when I had been sitting there for nearly fifteen minutes. The waiter, however, did not speak.

He just threw a large metal jug of water and four metal cups onto the table and returned to the table in the centre of the room. One of my dinner companions distributed the water. I pretended to drink it, but on the trip, I had been very careful of the water I drank and as I hadn't seen this water come from the larger water containers, I decided just to leave it.

Suddenly, all three men got up from the table, so I decide to follow them, like a lost puppy. They left the large green room and entered another smaller, greener room. I don't know why I followed them but something told me to. I tried not to make it that obvious and left a gap between the last man who got up and myself. As they entered the smaller room, I realised why they had all got up at the same time before they placing their order; they needed to wash their hands, and so did I. The hand washing place was separate from the toilets and there were at least eight sinks lined against the wall. Hand washing here in India is one of the necessary components of the eating process. I followed these men as they returned back to our table, still not a word or a gesture being exchanged. At last the waiter appeared and this time, I presumed he was there to take orders. The three men all spoke and ordered food; then it was my turn. I started to order rice and bread in Hindi, but remembered that I would not be understood.

I pointed to the three men that were now sitting opposite me and gestured that I would have the same as them. The waiter nodded and still the three men did not acknowledge me.

Then the food arrived: the jugs came and bowls were carried over to the table and I was given four different ladles of slop, one I recognised as dahl. The food was sloped out into the different sections on the metal plate. I looked at the food and didn't make any attempt to start eating it. I watched the men opposite, letting them take the lead, thinking I would attempt to copy how they were eating this liquid meal.

This was the first time that the men warmed to me and they smiled. They indicated what food I should eat first and how I should eat it. I copied, using my hands and fingers the best I could, utilising the chapattis as my main tool. I then waved my hand in front of my mouth to indicate to the men that I was finding this food very spicy. They smiled and I knew then that I would get further help from this in this eating experience. After nearly all the slop had been eaten, the rice appeared. I wondered why this did not come with the food at the start, but I have since found out this is normal practice for the way Indian food is served in India; I was just comparing my experience from the local tandoori that I had eaten in back in the UK. A pot of sugary milk arrived at the table. I tasted it but declined. I found it very difficult to eat sweet food mixed with savoury food, but that wasn't the case for the men opposite me, who seemed to be enjoying this milk mixed with the rice better than any other part of the food that had been served. I looked and, after I had declined the sugary milk, I still had some dhal left, but I had no bread left to help me eat it.

I looked across the table for some support and one of the men gave me a quick lesson on how to use the rice to help mop up the dhal. I had to mix the watery dhal with the rice with my fingers, using only one hand. It reminded me of mixing up some poly filler to fill a crack in the wall and my DIY skills had never been the best. I had to make sloppy round balls, which I attempted to make by chasing the rice and dhal around the plate. The men opposite were now laughing openly, watching me struggle. I finally make a ball of rice and dhal and then I had to consider how I would be able to transport this from the tray into my mouth. I considered 'living up' to my audience and thought about leaning my head back, opening my mouth and throwing the ball in. But, of course, I would do no such a thing and just continued to eat the sloppy balls the best I could. The meal was finished. I thanked the three men for their help, took a photo and washed my hands. I now had to pay. They indicated that I should follow them to a man sitting in the opposite corner of the room, behind a desk. Earlier I wondered what he was doing, but with everything going on, I had totally forgotten about him. He was the manager, the accountant and the cashier. I followed the three men who paid first. The total cost for my food and experience was 60 rupees, or around 80 pence. I left the green prison and the men left as well, all on one motor bike. I walked back to my hotel thinking this alien needs to be alone again.

Munna

Chapter 21
Heat, Eat and Feet

Day 18 and I had covered 276 kilometres on foot. This was an average of 16.23 kilometres a day. I wasn't sure if that was a good achievement, but considering I had spent nearly three days out of action with bad blisters, it was a total I could work with.

I was attempting to stop at a small village called Yedepolly, but whilst walking, I saw a sign showing that Nizamanbad was only twenty three kilometres away, so I decided to walk all the way there because it was a bigger town. This way I could be confident of finding accommodation. I was walking through a Muslim area and somehow it felt different. Not so many people stopped, so I thought I could be in for a less eventful day. I walked past a market, where a man was selling goats' heads. Entering Nizamabad, I was approached by a young man in a rickshaw, whose name I found out later was Prinz Arbanz. He had borrowed the rickshaw from his father who had sent him into to the market to get the shopping. So why not pick up a white man in a pink hat and try to give him a lift? All normal stuff. Prinz was a friendly young man and understood that, although I would not have a ride, I didn't mind getting in his rickshaw for a look.

He was so proud of it, even if it was his father's. But he understood I didn't need a lift into town because I was walking. This young man, like many I had met on trip, stayed in touch and phoned me many times later to see if I as ok. Soon I said goodbye and checked into a hotel, with nothing more unusual to speak about.

Morning came and it was the first morning that I was not bothered by barking dogs. I needed to get on a bus and have it to stop somewhere in the middle of nowhere, allowing me to achieve my day's walking. But again, normal communication problems meant that I almost had to fight with the bus conductor to stop the bus before it arrived all the way at my next destination. I had planned to walk about eighteen kilometres and, once off the bus, I thought that this would be easily achievable. But what with the lengthy communication problems, when I started to walk, I noticed time was moving on and the heat was becoming unbearable. I looked at my map and Google confirmed it was in fact eighteen kilometres to my next stop. I estimated that I could stop at Ankapoor, a small village, for more water, but that was at least seven kilometres away. Looking around, I noticed that I was now walking through a desert, with sand everywhere and hardly any greenery. It reminded me of Arizona in the US. I needed to walk through this desert to get to today's destination - a small town called Armoor.

More dead animal carcases seemed to by the side of the road than any other day I had been walking so far. I was stopped by a man on his bike; a farmer called Ravi, who reassured me that I could make it to Ankapoor to fill up on my water supplies. He was correct and when I struggled into the little village, I was so glad to see Ravi waiting by a small shack on his bike to make sure that I was OK. I don't think I have ever been so thirsty in my life; I drank two litres of water in no time and then bought another two to take with me. I looked at my watch, it was nearly 9.00am and the temperature was over 45°C. Due to the desert terrain, I really needed to be out of the sun by 10.00am, or 11.00am at the absolute latest. This was now a test of planning, and if I got it wrong, being alone, walking in such heat could be a matter of life or death. That might sound like an exaggeration, but for the first time, I really did feel worried, with the heat beating down and my water supplies running low. I could hear my wife saying '*John remember you are a school teacher, not an explorer.*'

Whilst drinking the much-needed water, Ravi kindly offered to phone up the lodgings in Armoor, thus giving me one less thing to worry about. I was too weak to argue with him and agreed. He wanted to give me a lift for the remaining seven kilometres, but I refused.

It would have been so tempting to say *yes* and jump on his bike. No-one would ever know. But I would know and even though I had accepted that I couldn't walk all the distance I had envisaged, I had given myself a daily target of a full day's walking and I wasn't going to go back on that if I could help it. Arriving in Armoor, I found the hotel that my farmer friend had phoned and happily, they were expecting me. I could have easily taken for granted all the help I had received along the way, but I made myself stop and think of each and every single act of kindness. I took each one on its own merits. Some people had helped me a lot; others might have just pointed me in the right direction. I knew that without all their help, I would not have made it so far. When the hotel manager said that Ravi had phoned and they were expecting me, I looked to the sky, put my hands together and silently thanked Ravi. Was this all luck, faith or just what can happen on an adventure? I didn't know, but I was thankful.After checking into the hotel, I was soon out on the streets, trying to find somewhere to eat. Everywhere I looked seemed like too much hard work. I was so tired that this eating business was not enjoyable. It was a necessary chore that had to be done quickly so I could get to bed and get ready for the next day's walking.

After my last meal in the green prison, I couldn't face a similar experience, so I was looking for something quick and simple. All around the world eating can be seen as a social thing, and so it should be. Going out for a meal on a first date, or gathering every evening to sit around the table with your family to eat and talk, what can be better? Unfortunately, that gathering for eating together is something that is being lost in the UK. I find that sad. With people working long hours and starting and finishing at different times of the day, the ritual of eating together is being lost. But here in India and especially since I have been walking, I have considered the whole process of eating in a different way.

A few years ago, a colleague of my wife's, an Ethiopian head teacher, came to stay at our house in the UK, and experiencing the way he ate made me consider eating in a different way. I will never forget what he said. When we asked him if he had enough food, he would reply that he was *satisfied*. (He also described cereal as *factory food* and turned his nose up at it, but that was a different matter). I never forgot how he would say he was *satisfied*, meaning that the food had served its purpose; nothing more and nothing less. That was sort of how I felt whilst walking or after I had finished a day's walking. I needed to eat but that was it. It wasn't a great part of my day; I didn't really look forward to it.

It could be described as the complete opposite of when you are on holiday in a foreign country. There, you are walking around, up and down romantic streets, browsing at menus before you decide, on that particular night, you fancied fish and you chose the restaurant with the smiley waiter who beckons you to come into his restaurant. Before you eat, you talk, you laugh you decide what to drink, then you decided on the fish, what sort of fish and how it should be cooked grilled or fried.

Here, there was no deciding or pleasure. I needed to eat quickly and with least amount of effort. After looking at a few different coloured prisons, it was the samosa stand again. Two samosas, two packets of biscuits, all washed down with a litre of cold water.

After eating, I needed to find a shop that sold shampoo, which I was going through really quickly, because not only was I using it to wash my whole body, I was also using to wash my clothes every night. I had to make sure the bottle was not too big as I didn't need to carry any excess weight. I also needed salt, which again, I was using every night to ease my blisters with, if I was lucky, warm water.

Sadly, most nights I only had access to cold water, so the salt water mixture obviously was nowhere near as effective. I had already used one and half kilograms of salt in three weeks. But I still soldiered on.

Prinz Arbanz

Chapter 22
SV and Naresh

Nineteen kilometres of walking were planned for today and I needed to get to the bus station.

After the now ever familiar communication problem, I boarded the bus and struggled to find a seat that could house me and my oversized rucksack. The bus conductor wobbled his way down the bus, as it bumped and swerved along the dirt track of a road; everyone sitting down holding on tight for dear life. The bus conductor arrived at my seat. I tried to pronounce where I wanted to get off the bus and he repeated it, looking at me, unable to understand why a white man with a massive rucksack and a pink hat would want to get off in such a small village in the middle of nowhere. I give him 50 rupees; the fare was 24 rupees, but he gave me back no change. I wondered why but he just moved on to the other people on the bus, collecting fares. I couldn't help but notice that he seemed to be giving everyone else change, so why not me? I converted the money and the change he owed me was less than 30 pence, so I tried to forget about it. But for some reason it didn't sit well and so far on this trip, hardly anyone had taken advantage of me; that in itself is a compliment to the country and its wonderful people. I was not going to let a flash young bus conductor get to me and affect my overall view of this country.

But still, it didn't sit well. I looked out of the window at the landscape and all I could see was desert, just like yesterday. Today though, I was better prepared, carrying three litres of water, two of them already diluted with hydration salts.

My stop arrived and I signalled to the bus conductor that I needed to get off. I thought about saying something to him about the change that was owed to me, but I decided it was not that important. I had to concentrate on getting off the bus, keeping all my belongings intact. But just as I was about to disembark, the conductor patted me on the shoulder and gave me my change. I thanked him and left the bus. The bus drove off. I wondered why he hadn't given me my change straight away as he did with all the other passengers. I was glad I had kept my mouth shut and hadn't said anything. I have found that just waiting to see what happens really works, especially in this country. I pulled the heavy rucksack onto my back, looked forward along the road, seeing just dust and a desert haze and I off I went, best foot forward. Whilst walking, I got a call from my wife Michelle who sounded a bit worried. She informed me that she had been watching the BBC news and it had been reported that central India was in the middle of a heat wave.That I already knew! Michelle went on to say that India had recorded some of its hottest temperature ever, in the areas I was walking through. She elaborated: several deaths had occurred in my area over the last few days, because of the heat.

I knew I had to be careful when walking in these temperatures and this conversation just made me more cautious.

The temperature was really getting to me and I could feel my already slow pace had decreased significantly. Walking, I was stopped by the normally interested people that passed me, most of them on motor bikes. Selfies were taken and lifts to the next town refused. Then I was stopped by two older men on a bike. I say older, they were both younger than myself. They both spoke good English and I explained my mission. One of the men told me he lived in the next town, not the one I was walking to today, but the town after that. He was happy to continue to talk by the side of the road and explained that he used to live in Mumbai. This was where I met SV and his good friend Naresh; a meeting that would later turn into a friendship that I will never ever forget. We exchanged numbers and they encouraged me to phone them when I reached their town of Korutla. Despite driving in the opposite direction, the men offered to take me to the town of Metipally, where I was planning to stay that night. Thanking them, I declined; there were only two kilometres left for me to complete my walking for the day and I was determined that I would finish the day by walking.

They smiled, we shook hands and they drove off. I had both of their numbers safely on my note pad (where I wrote important things whilst walking) and if the written information is important enough at the end of the day, it got transferred into my diary.

I thought that they seemed like really great people. Tomorrow I would certainly take them up on their offer of phoning them when I reached their town. Who knows what could happen? I continued the last two kilometres into town. Once more, I think about fate and how, just by walking at a certain time in a certain place, you could meet someone who could become your instant friend. The road became busy, the noises became louder and the overall pollution and chaos increased – I was nearing the big town. I put my head down and tried to finish the day's walking as fast as I could.

I had no idea what this town would be like. I thought that it would be probably much the same as the many I had walked through before and I had no idea where I would stay. Starting to think about asking someone where I could get lodgings for the night, I heard a shout.

'John Sir'. I looked around and saw a bike approaching me at top speed. 'You are not walking very fast, are you?'

It was SV and Naresh. I agreed with their comment, laughing. These men did not only speak great English, they had wonderful sense of humour. SV went on to say 'don't stay here in Metipally. Jump on the bike and I will drive you straight to my house where you can stay in Korutla'. I seriously thought about their kind offer but I refused, explaining that I needed to walk every day if possible; they both understood. But their efforts and kindness for the day did not stop there.

'Sir, if you will not drive straight to my house today, then you must let us make sure that we take you to a safe, cheap hotel', SV said. I agreed and jumped on their bike.

The men were true to their word and a cheap hotel was found: the manager of which was only too pleased that I decided to stay at his establishment. I said goodbye to my two friends, promising to call them tomorrow when I arrived in Korutla.

I managed to find a small restaurant that evening and then found myself ready for another night in a strange hotel. It was really hot in the room and because SV and Naresh were more concerned about the price, the AC was hardly working; I was in for a long night. I had also developed three more large blisters on my feet, so they needed to be burst with a needle then soaked in a bucket of salt water.

As it was only fourteen kilometres to the next town, where I had promised to phone SV. I decided that I would try to walk a bit quicker, and I was surprised that the newly burst blisters seemed to feeling fine. Reaching the outskirts of Korutla, where I should have made the phone call, I decided that I walk into the centre of town and reach the bus station before I phoned SV. Later, I would discover that I walked right past them about two kilometres on the outskirts of the town.

Shortly after my call, my two friends arrived at the bus station on their bike and were all smiles and pleased to see me. Commenting again on how slow I was walking, they had been expecting me to phone a lot earlier, especially considering I had already walked past them. SV then asked if I had breakfast, and apart from my daily banana at 4.00am I said no. The men looked around the bus station and soon we were all sitting down eating breakfast together – vegetable dosas. I offered to pay but they wouldn't let me. We spoke like we were old friends and it was a strange experience where it seemed as though I had met these men before, (and I am not talking about just yesterday). It was a strange feeling and I knew that these men would look after me, as a total trust had been formed.

Pinching myself to remind me how lucky I had been to have met them. Every time I meet such good people, I try not to take it for granted, thinking that this could be the last person I will meet for a while. Then someone else shows up and looks after me, feeds me; no better than the last person I had met, just different.

Breakfast finished, I jumped on their bike and SV took me to his office, a small building that from the front looked just like a garage.

I had walked straight past it on the other side of the road two hours previously. I had already met so many varied people with different occupation ranging from farmers to social workers, dentists to lorry drivers. It was becoming a bit of a game of mine, trying to guess the occupation of the next person I would meet that helped me. I thought back only a few days ago when Munna the typist had helped me. I wondered, what did these men do for a living?

As we approached SV's shop, I could get no clue as to what his occupation was. Looking at the door in a side garage, maybe a mechanic? No. It turned out that SV was a cement dealer and he explained that in India, a lot of cement was used.

In fact, India is amongst one of the largest users of cement in the world. He explained that he owned part of a factory that made the cement and he just used this shop to sell the cement to whoever he could, but not on a small scale; not to individual people who were interested in building a wall, but to large companies that were interested in building large apartment blocks.

I was fascinated as he talked. I asked if I could see the factory but he explained that it was too far out of town for him to take me. This was the first time that, as much as I had grown to like this SV, I wasn't sure he was telling me the complete truth, but I didn't care. I was safe, enjoying his company and hospitality and I had already had removed my boots and socks to get some air to my newly blistered feet.

Sitting on a comfortable chair, SV asked a man, who I assumed was his apprentice, to get a bucket of hot water, for me to soak my feet in. I explained that I already had some salt. SV showed great concern over the state of my feet and was really worried when I explained how many miles I still had planned to walk.

SV's grandfather turned up and we just sat and talked, his English being good enough for general conversation; SV translated anything that was a bit more difficult. We must have spoken for over an hour and the grandfather seemed like a nice gentleman. Later I discovered that he was not really SV's grandfather, just an old man that was his friend. It seems that once you become a good friend here in India, you take on family status, like brother, cousin, uncle or in this case, grandfather. Whilst I was sitting outside SV's office, Naresh, who was in real estate, left to go to work.

The sun was beating down and it was difficult to comprehend that being outside in the shade was cooler than sitting in the shop, which had no AC. My feet had been totally rested and as I sat there, I was wondering what adventures SV and Naresh had in store for me. Would I be staying around one of their houses? Would I have to find another hotel for the night? I spoke to SV and he told me that I would be staying at his house, but he had to do some work this afternoon so Naresh would look after me.

I did find this a bit strange because I thought all the work that SV had to do would be carried out from the shop I was sitting outside of. I also wondered how Naresh could look after me if he was not about. But then he arrived and all three of just got on the back of SV's bike and set off to SV's house.

The house was small and in a quiet neighbourhood just outside the centre of town. It had a garden courtyard and a lean-to outside on a concreted cement floor. Well, why wouldn't it have? After all, SV's business was to sell cement. I was told that I would be sleeping outside on this floor. That was not a problem. My only concern was the mosquitoes, but I was assured I had nothing to worry about and when I did finally go to sleep that night, they were right. I did not get bitten once. SV left, saying he would return soon. I was now in the company of Naresh, a larger man than SV. His English was better than SV's and soon we were in full conversation. First, I asked him why SV didn't live with his wife. He replied that she was not very nice and he was better living alone. I thought this was a strange thing to say about your friend's wife, especially to someone you had just met, but I didn't give it another thought. Perhaps I should have.

Time would tell. Naresh realised I needed to wash and showed me to a clean outside bathroom. Once showered, I explained that I needed to wash the clothes I had been walking in. After looking around the house, I noticed that it had a TV, so when I asked if there was a washing machine, I was surprised when Naresh laughed. He explained that no-one had a machine, but that didn't stop Indians from doing their washing. He asked me for my washing powder, and when I produced some shampoo, the laughter increased.

We both laughed, this helped secure our bond of friendship. Naresh said he would go out and buy me some washing powder, so we locked up the house and just around the corner, there was a small store, where someone was selling essentials out of their front door. Asking if I needed anything else, Naresh would not allow me to use my money to buy the washing powder.Back at the house, in the courtyard, Naresh went about his business of washing my clothes including, to my embarrassment, my dirty underwear and socks. I tried to explain that I wanted to do it, but when I attempted washing, Naresh started laughing and he simply couldn't watch me do such a bad job. He took over completely and showed me how to wash clothes the Indian way. I was amazed and videoed this action on my phone; this time it was my turn to laugh. But Naresh wasn't laughing and he was putting everything he had into this exercise and his feet where his main tool. He stamped on the clothes on the hard-concrete floor and used both feet in unison to bash out all the dirt, rinsed them, washed them with powder and then washed the washing power out.

This same foot process was repeated several times. I had to have a go and being a football player in my day, I thought I would be quite good at this way of washing. But alas, I wasn't. In fact, I was useless and Naresh laughed again. I used the fact that my feet had bad blisters on them as my excuse for such a poor effort, but we both knew that wasn't the truth. This way of washing was a skill and one that had taken years of practise to perfect.

When Naresh finally finished, he said 'I am the only Indian washing machine that is needed here!'

I felt at easy with these two great men I had met and, like other people I had met before, I could have easily had stayed in their company for days. Looking back, I sometimes wished that I had stayed in these people's lives for longer and I felt resentful that my walking and my goal of walking every day across this country was, time and time again, getting in the way of the adventures I was experiencing. However, as I've said before, if I hadn't been walking every day, I wouldn't have the opportunity to meet new friends and enjoying different adventures, so I knew I had to keep on moving.

Sitting in the lean-to on the cement floor of S. V's house, Naresh and I chatted, watching the washing dry, hanging on a line in the courtyard. We spoke like we had known each other for a long time.

This experience of befriending someone so quickly and being so familiar with them was happening more than I ever imagined possible. It was a strange feeling and one that you never experience unless you travel and put yourself in different situations where you are relying on people to help you to move on or even survive. Hemingway once said, "The best way to find out if you trust somebody is to trust them" and that is so true. These men didn't have to help me, but they had gone out of their way to help me and was I glad.

Naresh explained that his business as an estate agent was not good; no one was buying houses any more. I explained that his situation was occurring in UK and, in fact, all over the world. People had less money and were worried about taking on large risks, such as buying houses. I wondered if he was not selling houses, how was he was managing to survive and look after his family. He explained that when he was earning lots of money, he bought a farm with some land, just in case and now that the land and farm was his only source of income. I was intrigued. He explained that he had planted mango trees and they were producing great fruit. He went on saying that they only really produce in April, May and June, with the fruit from these three months yielding enough money to support his family for the rest of the year.

The time had passed quickly and SV had returned from whatever business he had had to attend to. All three of us sat in the lean-to, talking. Everyone was getting hungry and SV said that he would take me for lunch, but not before I explained my planned route to cross this country to them. These two men were intelligent and they wanted to look closely at my route. This was the first time that since I had left and even before I had left that someone really wanted to know my plans. I had always said that the beauty of this trip was the fact that it was totally unplanned. I had no idea where I would be going every night, how far I would be walking or where I was stopping.

I had already been taught by Prakash, that sleeping in a tent was not a good idea due to the risk of wild leopard attacks. These two men spoke to me with increased intensity and concern. I explained that I had no real plan and I was just walking across India following the route of the Godavari River the best I could. But this is when, just like the moment I had to get rid of the tent that my trip would take another turn. Showing them my future route, I could sense that they were worried, worried about my safety. I knew I had to listen and the fact that this trip had not been planned in great detail was a positive thing, easily allowing for necessary changes. Changes that could, in fact, have saved my life.

Not for the first time on my journey, I found myself sitting with people looking at old fashioned maps as well as modern maps on phones. I am always interested in taking people's advice and, as any traveller will tell you, it is wise to always listen to the locals and do what they would do. Looked intently at my so-called planned route, both men were very sombre.

They explained that the route I had half planned for the next few days was too dangerous for me to be undertaking, travelling alone. I was a bit puzzled and I explained to them that I had no attention of sleeping under the stars, but death by wild animal was not the danger.

What could be more dangerous than a snake or leopard attack? They explained that the town further along on my route was dangerous and only yesterday, thirty five people had been killed in a terrorist attack. I was a bit shocked at this news and was unaware that such incidents were occurring in this safe country. I really didn't know if I believed what they were saying, but I felt I was in no position to take any such risks. Naresh explained that most of the incidences that occur in this region were never reported on the news. I listened to them and was prepared to take on board what I had been told. They also stated that not only was this a bad area for terrorism but, due to its remote location, it was also a popular place for kidnappings.

I had thought I might have had a few problems trying to walk through this part of rural India, but until now, I had not given much thought to what type of problems they may have been.

After the towns of Chennur and Sironcha, there was nothing but forest for miles and hardly any villages at all. Naresh said that the villages in this forest area would not be able to accommodate me, having nowhere to sleep.

This was not the first time that I had encountered such problems and I was sure I could find somewhere, or someone, that would provide safe accommodation. But both of them were adamant, saying 'no, John Sir, please promise you won't walk through such areas.' Naresh explained that even if I avoided the terrorist areas and walked through the villages, there would not be enough water for me to get from one village to another. I looked both of these men in the eyes and thanked them. I didn't know how I was going to get around this problem, but I certainly wasn't going to go gung-ho, ignoring their advice with the chance of not making to the other side of this country.

I didn't want to appear worried about what they had told me, but on the other hand I didn't want to appear blasé either. These were great people and I just wanted to enjoy their company. The terrorist area and the forest were still a few days away; I would give this problem more thought when I got closer.

They had suggested I catch a train and just cut a large part of my journey out, get to the other side of the forest and continue walking from there.

This didn't sit well with me and I had already found it hard to come to terms with the fact that it was impossible to walk all the way every day, due to the lack of accommodation.

I needed to give this some serious thought and was sure, with a few solid days on my own, walking, I would come up with the correct solution. Perhaps this was a situation I could leave with my subconscious mind to sort out?

Thankfully, the conversation of wild forests and terrorist attacks was pushed aside and we left SV's house, returning to his shop, where I was introduced to more of his friends. Back on the bike once more, with another of his friend's, we went off to see a local lake. This was a tranquil spot and I was impressed with the colour of the deep green, caused by a type of algae. From the lake, SV pointed out that you could see Naresh's house. It was a new brown structure, and it was huge, definitely the largest house in town. I thought the estate agency business must have paid for that. No way could it have been the mango farm.

Lunchtime and we sat opposite each other in a small shop, with SV's bike parked outside. After washing our hands in the outside sink, it was time to eat. SV ordered and my fingers were employed again. A strange sensation of forever happiness passed onto me as I sat with this man, something that I had never experienced before. I just knew I had met a person I would know for the rest of my life, a friend. He smiled at me as if he could almost read my mind.

SV was a small man in stature, but had a huge personality. Everyone knew him and it seemed everyone had time for him. I thought he was about my age; I later found out he was a few years younger, but he didn't look it. As happy as he appeared and as friendly as he was, there was something behind those telling brown eyes that was worrying him. Something that made him appear older than his years. I had now seen him on three separate occasions and every time, he wore such colourful flowery shirts that made his personality stand out even more. But there was something there, deep inside him that just didn't run true. This strange sensation that I felt towards him in no way made me doubt him as a friend, as a person. He had a wonderful personality, great manners and kind ways. I wanted to know this man more. Who knows: perhaps if we stayed friends after this trip, I could come back and visit him and really find out what and how, this man ticked, even perhaps help him in some way? What a strange feeling to get. How I could help SV? He was the one helping me?

After lunch he drove me around town meeting more of his friends and showing me off to anyone he could. I sat on the back of his bike, feeling really safe and lucky to have met another great person who was helping me on my journey. He then said that he wanted to show me a house that he owned and that he was trying to sell.

This was the moment when the alarm bells started to ring; this was the moment when all the thoughts I had had toward him were indeed getting more mysterious by the hour. Was he just a good business man who had his fingers in many pies or was there something he was telling me? I walked around an empty house and he explained that he would be selling this house for nearly double for what he had paid for it. I was confused I thought he was in the business of selling cement. I said nothing and just enjoyed his company.

It was getting dark and after looking around the empty house, he introduced me to another of his friends. He drove me to this man's shop, who sold everything you could possibly imagine - most of it made of plastic. This man, along with everyone in the shop, was pleased to see SV.

After walking around the plastic hardware shop, it was back on his bike to meet another friend, this time a currency seller. But not before he had haggled to buy a water melon from the back of a huge truck parked in the middle of the town. The currency dealer was a friendly man and was interested in my mission and, in fact, after this meeting, he followed my blog all the way to the end.

After this final introduction, SV and I just strolled through town and headed back to his house. It was at this moment I had a strange thought about meeting SV by chance, whose real name was Vinayak Sabbani Rao.

I did then wonder why he was called SV and not VS - maybe just another thing to add to the mystery of this man. I thought back over the last weeks and all the people that I had been lucky enough to meet. It had been a week since I had met Sarang, the social worker; then Sharad, the young farmer and his cousin, Sachin. Further back, I had met the first Satis, the man who had taken part in the *Who Wants to be a Millionaire* competition and then the another Satis and his daughter, who had shown me around a temple on the banks of the Godavari. Nearly, but not all, the wonderful people I had met so far had names that began with the letter *S*. How odd, I thought. Back at SV's house, I was ready for sleep. This had been another full-on day for me, but SV was still interested in talking. He was explaining what great investments could be made in this town, and how land in Korutla had increased in price more than Mumbai. I was still a bit confused as I thought that his friend Naresh was the real estate guru. He then said that people in Mumbai have invested lots of money in this town and this was the place to earn money by buying and selling houses. To me, Korutla seemed like a great place in some ways different from many of the towns that I had walked through, but a place to earn money? I wasn't sure anyway and what would I know? In fact, what did I care? However, SV did seem a little obsessed by this way of making money, which again seemed a bit strange because everything about this man did not once seem to indicate that he was money driven in any way.

He stated that what someone could earn in Mumbai in one month a person could live on that money all year in rural India. He said that the gap between rural and urban India had to change and he indicated that it was this fact that money could be earned from it. I suppose a little bit like the North/South divide back in the UK. I tried to act interested, but all this money talk so late in the day was a bit much for me. I tried to change the subject and to talk about his family. I asked about his wife and children he had mentioned to me earlier, but he didn't really want to talk about them. He told me that his wife lived with her family, and he didn't see her or his children that much. For such a good man, that seemed very sad. It is not uncommon in India for the wife to return to her family for large periods of time before returning back to her husband and the marital home. Without prompting, SV spoke how his wife's family were rich and he had worked in Dubai with them, but he didn't want follow the money. There was genuine sadness in his eyes as he told me this. This was another moment when what S.V was saying didn't really add up. If he wasn't interested in chasing the money in Dubai, why was he so interested in chasing money, buying and selling properties here in a small town in the middle of India? He looked me straight in the eyes, as if he was looking into my soul and I felt he was going to tell me there and then all about the real SV, all the things that really didn't add up, but just as he took a seat on the floor next to me in the lean-to and was about to get serious, Naresh appeared.

The moment was gone and, sadly, it was gone forever. Naresh came dancing into the house. It seemed obvious that he had been partying ever since I had left him earlier that day. He had been drinking heavy and not just chai.

Naresh offered me an alcoholic drink and, in a normal situation I would have found nothing more enjoyable than sinking a few with this man. But I turned the offer down, as I had remained totally dry ever since the walk had started. I was tempted but, like every day, I needed to be 100% fit and ready for the whole day of walking that lay ahead of me. Naresh totally understood. Food was prepared, mainly consisting of rice, which I refused at such a late hour and only ate a banana. Despite being under the influence, Naresh made sure that I had remembered his advice and would not be walking through the terrorist areas and deserted forest. I was getting tired and I needed to sleep. I blew up my inflatable mattress that had been a god send and had saved my back on many occasions, but would come in particularly useful tonight as I prepared to sleep outside on a cement floor. Naresh left and I settled down to sleep on the floor next to SV. I reminded him that I needed to be up and on the road about 4.30am. He replied that that was not a problem and he would drop me at the bus station in the morning. The first bus would leaving at 5.30am and I needed to be on it.

SV wanted to talk more as we lay on the floor, but the tiredness had kicked in. I am sure he wanted to tell me his full story, but I just did not have the energy to listen.

He explained that he would be up at 3.00am to mediate and if I heard him or saw him in the night, not to be alarmed. I thought to myself what else will I learn, or find odd about this wonderful man? In fact, during the night I did look over to see if S.V was ok and I could see him crossed legged sitting up mediating, I was fascinated.

My alarm woke me and I heard a noise of something running over the lean-to roof. SV soon woke after me. I assumed he must have gone back to sleep after he had meditated. I looked up to the roof, and to be honest, I was a bit frightened by what I could see and hear. Whatever was on the roof it was large and it wasn't on its own. The noise-makers showed themselves: grey monkeys that looked like baboons, the same type of monkey that attacked me on my first day. Without warning SV jumped out of bed and grabbed a nearby stick and chased them out of his garden. He said they were a problem and often came up to his house and even into the house if he left the doors open by mistake.

Getting ready to leave, we spoke like old friends. SV made some lemon tea and after he had chased the monkeys away for a second time, he put food out for the birds to eat. I thought there was something always special about a person that has time to think about feeding the birds.

Tea finished, SV told me that he had a special treat for me. I was wondering what he could have in store for me. Whilst packing away my bed and prepared my feet for another day's walking, SV went into the house, returning to the lean-to with a tin. It was an old tin; it looked like something your aunty would keep her biscuits in and only get out on special occasions, a birthday or Christmas. He said he would like to give me some herbal tea, which used to be his father's and the tea was maybe thirty to forty years old. I was honoured and accepted this kind gesture. While drinking the tea, he spoke more about his father, who had long passed away. He told me that his father was a great spiritual leader, and was highly thought of; he said that he had healing powers. He then said that it was his father that had got him into meditation, and he had been waking up and mediating in the middle of the night every day of his life since he was thirteen years of age. I was in awe of what I was hearing. I had often wondered about mediation and it was at this point, that mediation entered my life.

Gathering my things, I looked at SV and out of all the great people that I had met so far, this man fascinated me the most. I wanted to stay in his company and get to know him better. I really wanted to find out why certain things he had shared about his life didn't add up.

But again, I couldn't. I was driven on by my adventure. Just before we left his house, he showed me a photograph of him as a teenager with his mother and father. It was in black and white and had been enlarged and it was also laminated. I looked at the photograph and I could see the similarities between him and his father. It was a great photograph and I could tell by the way he smiled and looked at it, he was so proud of it. I thought that he must come from a wealthy family, for them to have been able to afford to have such a photograph taken in India at that time. I held it in both my hands and tried to feel the history, SV studying my expression. I asked if he had the original and he said no. Then he said 'John Sir, I would like you to take this with you on your travels. It will look after you and if you keep it safe, it will forever keep you safe'.

I knew that there was no way I could take the last photograph of him and his family, so I refused, as politely as I could. I nearly cried that he had offered this to me as a gift. I believed that this was the most important possession he owned and he had wanted to give it to me, to keep me safe. I had said no, but later, I wished I had said yes.

On the way to the station on the back of SV's bike, I felt so good.

I can't explain how or why had felt so good. I have never taken drugs, but people tell me that when you first take drugs it feels so good it's hard to explain. I am not suggesting that the herbal tea had a drug like effect, but I did feel more alive and energised at 5.00am in the morning than I had done the entire trip. Maybe I felt so happy to have met such a man or maybe I felt lucky that I was able to be involved in such an adventure, where meeting people was taking all the prizes over completing the walk.

Before we parted, he stopped on the side of the road and bought me some more tea. Then from his pocket he produced another tin, one a lot smaller than the tin that held the herbal tea. What else could this man do that would surprise or fascinate me more? He then opened the tin and, whilst we were drinking tea on his bike, he told me to hop off, so I did. He then opened the tin and I put down my plastic cup. He told me to look at him. I did and he produced some powder from the tin and blessed me. I had to hold the tears back.

'Now, John Sir, you are turning into an Indian'.

I finished the tea; we embraced each other and then parted. I walked towards yet another crowed Indian bus station.

SV and Naresh

Chapter 23
Johnny Arrives

The reality of the long walk that I had in front of me was glaring me in the face when I woke up. Meeting such great people makes it easy to forget that I still had a lot of walking ahead of me. I was here to walk across India and that is what I needed to focus on. This morning, my walking boots were causing the problem. On the left foot, there was a tear on the canvas. I looked at it and seriously thought that maybe I had chosen the wrong footwear. I had long thought about taking my leather boots that I had had for a few years, but decided that it would be too hot to wear them. Instead, I had opted for a lighter pair of walking boots that would allow my feet to breathe. At this point, holding the boot in my hand, I felt I had made the wrong decision. It's amazing how resourceful you have to become when there are no shops and no Tesco where you can get want you want, when you want. I knew that I had to fix my boots now or, at least, stop the rip from getting any bigger. These boots, just like my rucksack, had become almost part of me and, without either, I would not be able to complete my task. One thing I did have lots of was plasters and, as I was using them daily on both of my poor feet, I thought if applied them to my boots every day perhaps this would prevent the tear from spreading and stop the possibility of my foot sneaking its way out of the side of the boot.

I plastered my boots up for the first time that morning and, like lots of things on this walk, just hoped for the best.

I got off another bus and started walking again; with five hours of solid walking, I had estimated I would reach the next town before midday. The phone rang.

'Hello John Sir'.

It was Habil, the lorry driver that I met two weeks ago.

'Are you OK? Are you in Mumbai yet?'

'Hello Habil, I am in Korutla'

'Ah, good, thank you, bye'.

Since meeting Habil, he had phoned me every single day. Sometimes he would phone twice a day; sometimes three times. I only had to say I was OK and then he would ring off. This really touched me, I did wonder if he only phoned me to practice his English, but thinking about the limited daily conversation, I believed he was just checking in with me.

I was heading for the next town called Jagitial and this is where I was meeting Johnny that evening. Jonathan Ball, Johnny, was nineteen years of age and was the son of one of my wife's closest (and oldest) friend, Josie. Josie had come to visit us in Mumbai earlier in the year and was blown away by India and its people. During her stay, she visited both my wife's school and my slum school. Explaining that I was planning to walk across India to raise money for the children I was teaching, Josie showed genuine interest in my trip.

She asked if I would be walking alone and I said that I would be. She inquired if I would be interested in someone joining me for part of the walk. I was up for anything and when I started to plan this adventure, at some point I hoped I might be joined by some of the many people that were supporting me from the UK. Josie went on to explain that Jonathan, her son, would love to come and walk part of the way with me and so the seed was sown. I had met Johnny a few times and had, over the years, seen him develop from a child into a teenager and then into a man. I remember the first time I met him, which was at his house in Southport. He had great delight in showing me his dinosaurs and train set; he was five, maybe six years of age.Prior to the trip, when I was last in the UK, I went around and met him. I think he was expecting a detailed schedule of events, but as he sat on the sofa with his mother Josie next to him, I explained there was no proper schedule and there were no real plans.I described how I wanted to do the walk the old-fashioned way. I wanted to attempt this with no set plan, just a determination to get to the other side.
I explained that years ago, before maps and certainly before Google, explorers just set off. OK, I omitted the fact that some died on the way. He looked at me as if I was mad: 'so you are walking across India following the Godavari River on your own with no plan and no time scale'. I said 'yes'
That seemed about right. Not only was I going to walk across India with no plan on my own, but was he mad enough to fly out and join me? He replied the same 'Yes'.

However, we did Google Map the river whilst I was there in Southport and his one comment was: 'this does look a little remote in places. Where will you sleep?

My answer: 'I have no idea'.

As I walked the road, thinking how good it would be to have company and be able to talk in normal English to someone, I was getting excited and just wanted to get to the town as soon as I could. The usual things that occurred most days repeated themselves. Lots of men on bikes stopped me on the side of the road, offering me a lift. I would refuse, have a selfie, one of possibly fifty taken that day and continue to walk. Then, just by chance, a man stopped and he looked familiar. 'Do you remember me?', he asked and to be totally honest, I didn't but I said that I did.

 I had met so many people who had stopped on the side of the road, offering me help; he was just one of many men. He said that he had met me on the road three days ago. He then got his phone out and showed me the evidence - a picture of a white man wearing a pink hat and him, both smiling. We laughed, so just by chance he saw me again, three days further along the long road across this country. Then, to make this situation even stranger, he asked me:

'Sir, are you Indian?'

I looked at him and thought that he must be joking. Was he trying to offend me? What a strange question to ask a pale, if not a little sun burnt, foreigner if I was Indian. Then I realised I still had the bhindi on my forehead, from yesterday when SV had blessed me. We laughed even more. Like the first time, he asked if I needed a lift and just like the first time, I refused. He told me it was only five kilometres into town and that I should be manage to get there before it became too hot. Thanking him, we parted for the second time.

Later arriving into town, this same man was sitting on his bike waiting outside the bus station. I said hello again and this time he insisted that I jump on the back of his bike and he would take me to the best hotel. I agreed; it was only two minutes around the corner. He helped me off and arranged my night's accommodation. Then, just like the two previous times I had met him, he was gone. I wondered if I would bump into him again.

My current situation was now a bit different; I didn't just need to book a room for one. Tonight, I needed a twin room with two beds; the hotel manager wondered why. But I didn't have the energy to tell him I was being joined by someone else from the UK.

What I lacked in height, Johnny certainly made up for it. He was over six-foot-tall and very slim in stature. Dark eyes, dark hair. I suppose he was like most 19 years old, but at first, I found it difficult to see past his tall, gangly appearance. He was full of an energy, but his energy was for adventure which was different to mine. He had found himself with me in the middle of rural India without really knowing what to expect. But he was up for whatever the next few days with me would give him.

I remember going travelling for the first time at the age of twenty and that experience was something that has stayed with all my life. I kept telling him to just take in as many of these different experiences as you can. It won't be until you return home, that you will look back on this time and know that this experience will have changed the way you operate and think. When he agreed with me, I am sure that he was just agreeing to keep me quiet and I don't really think he could imagine what would happen to him over the next few days that followed. I didn't either.

'Hi John, it's Johnny. I think I am outside the hotel' was what I heard when I answered the phone.

'Great, I am coming down'.

At the tender age of nineteen, Johnny had decided to join me on my walk and I was grateful. He had come via Mumbai, where he had stayed in our Chembur apartment. My wife had picked him up from the airport. Later he said that he didn't enjoy Mumbai and he could not get used to the mass of people, the filth on the streets and the air pollution. After spending only one night there, he had caught a flight to Hyderabad, the closest big town with an airport to my location. From there, he had negotiated a driver to bring him to this small town of Jagital. It was a long drive from Hyderabad to Jagital and he had had problems finding a driver that was willing to take on this fare. I think the driver had probably taken more money from Johnny than he should have, but Johnny didn't care. He was safe and he had made it.

We hugged and Johnny looked tired, amazed, excited and in shock as if all of these emotions had joined together into one. He looked at me as if to say 'I made it' but was certainly living in the present and, as he stood on the street outside our hotel, he couldn't relax. He was looking in every direction all at once, trying to take in all the strange sounds, smells and noises, mainly from the traffic. He talked about his journey in great detail, describing the driver and his long drive to reach me.

But as he spoke, he moved, he was a big male from Merseyside but here he was a fish out of water. I can remember when I first experienced culture shock when I was travelling alone at twenty one through Indonesia and I didn't know at the time if it felt good or bad. I think it just felt strange and I remember being annoyed with myself that I wasn't able to take in all that was happening at once. This was now happening to Johnny and I was there to watch it happen. It was almost funny to see. It was 9.30pm and by now on a normal day's walking, I would have already been asleep for hours, but I knew this could be a long night. Johnny explained in great detail how, while he was waiting outside the hotel, many strange men had approached him. He said one had just come up and given him a mango and then wanted to look at his phone. He said he hadn't minded until the man wanted to see a picture of his girlfriend. At that point, he told him to get lost, but he still kept the mango! We laughed and tried to come to terms with how he and I were standing outside a street shack, eating samosas in a small town in rural India. The answer was that we couldn't really work out how we had got to this point, except that I was on a mission and he had decided he wanted a small part of that. But not for the fund raising or the same reasons that had motivated me; he wanted a part of this adventure purely for himself and he wanted to take the opportunity to walk in parts of India that western people just hadn't walked through before.

I explained to him that for safety reasons and to save money, we would be sleeping in the same room every night. He looked at me in a strange way and I confirmed that all hotels have more than one bed in a room. I not sure that they did, but I didn't want to worry him with the fact that he had to share a bed with a fifty-year-old that he really didn't know that well. We were going to be living and sleeping together and he had to be aware that this was the situation. I didn't know if he had even thought about the physical situation of where and how we going to sleep, but either way, he had to know and it was vital that we both felt comfortable in each other's company.

I helped him up to the room, where the two large double beds were pushed together and he was ok with this arrangement for the night. We spoke and I probably tried to talk him to death because I had not spoken to anyone western for weeks. He listened and we laughed. I then explained that we would have to get up at 4.00am every morning because we needed to do a full day's walking before it became too hot. The idea of him getting up this early shocked him and if he enjoyed his teenage years anything like mine, the only time he would normally see 4.00am was when he was coming home from a night out. Turning the lights out, I said I needed to go to sleep. He said that was not problem and he left the room to go outside to contact his girlfriend and mum back in the UK to say he had met up with me and he was safe.

I knew that there would be no problems between the two of us: we would get on and now being two, a different sort of adventure awaited us both.

Johhny

Chapter 24
Shiva Me Timbers

I was worried that Johnny might struggle with the very early start the next morning, but after a few shakes, he was up. He lay on the bed and looked in amazement as I began the dressing of my feet. I told him not worry it as took a lot of weeks for my feet to get in such a bad way. Anyway, he wouldn't be walking long enough for his feet to get anywhere near as bad as mine. I also explained that the boots needed morning treatment as well. One of the reasons that I had to get up so early, other than battling against walking in the sun, was the time it took to get my feet ready for walking. The boy did well and soon we were out of the hotel, making our way to the bus station. I explained to him that the distances between the towns where we could find sleeping accommodation were too far to walk in one day, so on many days, I had to catch a bus and get dropped off in the middle of nowhere, leaving me to walk into the next town. I think he understood and took this news in a positive light; he appeared to be ready for his first day of walking.

I really didn't know how good or bad Johnny was going to be at this walking business, so I thought I would play it safe and only walk about fifteen kilometres on his first day and see how he coped. As always, my main concern was the temperatures. And I know, because I have spent lots of time in his (and my wife's) home town of Southport, that even on a hot summer's day, compared to this, Southport would be considered cold. I now didn't only have to worry about my own safety; I had to look after Johnny, as I promised his mother that he would return to Merseyside in one piece. But I was happy to do this. It was so good to have company, and someone that understood what I was saying. It had been nearly four weeks for me without this simple privilege.

Starting to walk, we were soon watching the sun come up over the best scenery I had seen so far. Johnny was overwhelmed with what he was seeing; he never thought that walking through this part of central India would be so beautiful. I thought to myself that usually it wasn't, but as luck would have it, he had joined me in a scenic area: buffalo ambling across the road, herds of them, controlled by farmers and dogs. We were taking so many photographs that it was getting in the way of the walking.

Johnny, being such a tall man, was naturally a faster walker than me and even on this first day of us walking together, he would find himself a long way ahead of me. If we were not talking in the hours that we walked, he would go ahead and, at times, we wouldn't be together and it was like we were walking on our own. He would stop after a while and I would catch him up.

As we walked, we talked and I wondered whether we would get as much attention from the locals with there now being two of us, rather than just me on my own. I thought there was no way as many people would stop to offer their help to two men compared to one on his own. But, more people stopped during the course of the walk that day; fifty or more in fact. I explained to Johnny that people stop because they most likely want to help; they are curious or mostly, they just want a selfie with a white man who is lost. I told him that some people stopped and offered to give me a lift, but that most of the time, I refused. On some occasions, however, for the experience, I accepted. I told Johnny about the rides I had taken, in all sorts of transport during the walk, but only after I had walked a certain distance first. After all, I am supposed to be walking across India, not hitching.

I didn't know why, but that day, I thought a tractor would stop, and I told Johnny that. He just looked at me as if to say *why? That's a bold statement.* We walked on through several villages, being swamped by friendly locals all wanting to know why we were walking. What must have we looked like? One tall man, one short man, both wearing the same grey T shirts advertising my mission, wearing ladies' hats. Mine was a lovely pink, (and you know the story behind that); Johnny had borrowed his mother's hat, which she had bought on her visit to India; it was a lovely white colour, decorated with flowers. I could say we resembled those two unfunny women/men that appeared on TV back in the 80's called *Hinge and Bracket*!

'Why do think a tractor will stop, J?'

We had decided that, when we first met up, that if your name began with J and to stop us both calling each other John, that J would do. It seemed like a good idea at the time.

'I don't know why J; I just have a feeling it will.'

We continued with the heat picking up. We had been walking for nearly fifteen kilometres and I was conscious of Johnny not being used to this walking lark, even though he was more than capable and obviously a lot, lot younger than me. Amazingly, just as I predicted, a tractor pulled over and, before we knew it, we were sitting in the back which was loaded full of corn.

Johnny couldn't believe it and even though I had predicted it, we were both a bit shocked. We lay amongst the grain, thinking how and why did this happen?

Trying to explain to him that a lot of things like this had happened to me on this walk, Johnny knew that I wasn't religious in any way. I told him that it seemed as though that someone or something was making sure that I was OK. Conveying to him that you did not have to be religious to have faith, I explained that I had always had faith and with what I had experienced during this trip, I now had more faith than ever. I am not sure Johnny understood what I was talking about and he gave me a look as if he really didn't care what I was talking about. But I tried to explain there were simply too many wonderful things happening for this just to be a normal situation, or for all of it to be just a series of coincidences. I think he thought I had just spent too much time alone, in the baking sun and with one foot following the other for nearly four weeks, he concluded that I had slowly gone mad.

We didn't stay long with the tractor and were soon walking again, being stopped by every other motor bike or person we passed in the villages. After about four hours of walking and socialising, we reached the outskirts of the town we were going to stay in that night.

Another vehicle stopped this time, a large 4X4 jeep. The man driving poked his head out of the window and said he would like to help us and show us around. We refused the lift, but I took his number anyway. His name was Shiva. He invited us to his brother's wedding, even though he'd just met us.

We inquired further about his brother's wedding, thinking we could stay and attend, but Shiva told us it was in two days' time, so we had to decline and get back walking.

We found a great hotel with AC and Johnny named it The Ritz. Compared to where we had stayed the previous night, when Johnny had arrived late from the airport, this hotel was a palace.

I asked him how he was feeling after the long walk and he replied that the walking itself was ok, but everything else that had happening was overwhelming. We had just settled into the room when I heard some drumming and loud music playing outside. I thought it was a wedding but I was wrong – it was a funeral.

I managed to get a photograph of the long parade of people that trailed behind the dead body as it was paraded through the streets. Johnny jumped off his bed and like me, saw the corpse. He just looked at me as if to say, 'how many more new experiences will I encounter in my first day's walking?' But this was only just the start; the day just kept going and going.

As we had arrived in the town earlier, I had noticed a barbers shop, a real Sweeney Todd's. I mentioned to Johnny that maybe later, we should get our haircut as it would be a laugh and he agreed. So, there we were, a haircut and a shave for both of us, costing less than £1.50. We both agreed afterwards that this was one of the best haircuts either of us had ever had.

After the barbers, we returned to the hotel with almost no time to eat. Needing to relax and thinking about getting an early night, I could sense Johnny's jet lag was catching up with him. It could have been the walking, or all the new experiences he was enjoying, or a combination of all three. Whatever the reason, he was getting tired, even though it was still very early in the day. I suggested that we took a short time to relax before we thought about sleep and he agreed.

But this never happened. Shiva phoned and told us he was coming to get us. He was here from Mumbai for his brother's wedding and wanted to show us around. First of all, he bought us ice creams and water and then drove us to his family's home where food was made especially for us. He explained that his family owned a timber yard and sawmill, which we were able to look around. Hence the name given to this chapter.

With his sister, we were driven down to see the Godavari River; it was so dry. The river almost looked like it had died. Shiva explained that this happens every summer and then the monsoon comes and the river comes back to life. I wanted to take so many photographs; I had never seen a river so dry and it was a ten-minute walk from the river banks before we were able to see any sign of water. This great river that I was following looked like it would never recover. The white and sand stone of its dry banks created craters that looked like they were from a different planet or even the moon. Temperatures were over fifty degrees. I had experienced heat like this whilst walking through the desert areas a few days ago, but somehow this seemed more intense and drier. The heat was so intense that my phone and camera wouldn't operate properly.

We couldn't stay out in this heat for long and Shiva, who had already shown us his love for an ice cream or two, was struggling to walk the ten minutes from the bank to the river's water. He had his head covered in a scarf and was complaining it was too hot for him; he was from Mumbai and not use to being out in the midday sun.

Walking back to the car to get out of the heat, I noticed a fire burning on the banks of the river. Shiva explained this was a funeral pyre and the body was being burnt. It was the same body we had seen earlier from the balcony of the hotel.

I wanted to look closer, but Shiva said that it was not culturally correct to go too close. Johnny and I looked at each other; this was the first time for either of us to smell the burning of human flesh. We practically ran back to the luxury of Shiva's 4X4 jeep and its air conditioning.

Off once more in the car, where we discovered that Shiva had planned a boat trip. Stopping by the side of the road, we were soon joined by the whole village as Shiva bought us sugar cane juice. What a man! We had only just met him and he was treating us like royalty. He asked us to stop thanking him, as this was what travelling was all about - people helping other people. So true, I thought. I hope I could return the compliment one day.

Having set off in the direction of the boat ride, Shiva discovered that it was closed. That didn't deter him; the boats maybe closed, but a temple visit was suggested instead.

We approached the temple and were overwhelmed by people wanting to show us around. After this temple experience, it was time to get away from the crowds and return back to the safety of the hotel. This is what it must feel like to be famous, I mused. We said goodbye to Shiva who was planning to meet us again tomorrow. But before he left, he went out to buy bananas and water for us.

Johnny lay on the bed speechless. I just smiled and we were just about to call it a day, when Shiva phoned to say he'd got our bananas and water, but also that the local press was with him. They wanted to interview me there and then. I put the phone down, nudging Johnny who was nearly asleep.

'J', I said, 'the press is here and they're coming up to our room right now'. Johnny quickly got off the bed and sorted out his hair.

They interview lasted for 10 minutes with Shiva acting as translator and before they left, he gave us the bananas and water.

The following morning, we had to catch a bus to the next village. An old man got on the bus, looked at me and then looked again. It was then that I noticed that a great many people on the bus seemed to be staring at us. Being the odd one out in this location, I didn't give it a second thought. Closely inspecting the newspaper that he was reading, the old man showed me a page and, lo and behold, there we were - Johnny and I - immortalised in the press of a local Indian paper.

From the interview the night before in our hotel room, we had made the local press.

I looked at the pictures of Johnny and I sitting on our hotel bed, thinking this was a bit like a scene out of one of the Harry Potter films, on the train, where the people featured in the articles were 'alive' - well, except that our pictures didn't move and didn't speak. Unbelievable!

Soon the whole bus knew we were famous and were aware of the good reasons we were walking. We got off the bus to start that day's walk and everyone on the bus shook our hands and clapped us. We waved as the bus continued on its journey, put our rucksacks on and started to walk.

Walking all day, we came to an enormous bridge that crossed the Godavari. Here, the river was the widest I had seen it since I had crossed it at the Dam. It was difficult to believe that in just one day's walking, we could see such a contrast in the river.

From being completely dry, it had changed to being nearly two kilometres wide. Crossing the bridge, we both took lots of photograph in between being approached by the usual bikes and cars for the obligatory selfies. We found a hotel and just as we were going to relax and eat before getting some sleep, the phone rung, it was Shiva – again - telling us he was on his way to collect us. Once more we found ourselves in the back of his 4x4. I asked Shiva what he did for a living back in Mumbai. He said he owned a business making and exporting electric bikes.

I smiled and thought to myself that here is another person I have met, with yet another occupation and whose name began with *S*. As we drove, I realised we were heading back to the village we had stayed in yesterday. At this point I tried to work out something that made no sense. I was going backward on this forward walk across India. This could not be good logic and I realised that if I was following sound logic, I would not have even started such a mad trip in the first place. Driving into the village where we had spent the whole of yesterday, we were becoming accustomed to the roads and the shops. It wasn't long before Shiva had stopped at the same ice cream shop and bought us ice cream, followed by more bananas and water. It seemed that Shiva had no real plan, he just wanted to spend time with us and, after completing another full day's walking, just sitting in the back of his air-conditioned jeep felt fine to us. Driving along, we saw a man climbing a tall cocoanut tree using his feet, just like a monkey would. We asked Shiva what he was up to and he told us he was collecting tree juice. SV had mentioned tree juice to me the other day and had offered to let me try some. On that occasion, I declined. But now Shiva was not going to give me that option. Stopping his jeep, he told the man up the tree to come down as he wanted to buy some of this tree juice. The man slid down this fifty-foot tree in about two seconds and quickly got the plastic cups ready for us to try it. It was alcoholic and very popular in these parts. In fact, we had encountered a man on a motor bike earlier in the day who, despite weaving all over the road, still offered us a lift. We obviously declined and I remarked to Johnny then that I thought he had been on the tree juice. It tasted bitter and sweet at the same time, with an awful after taste. You could taste the alcohol and because I had been totally dry on this trip, it made it taste even worse. I think Johnny was more up for this experience than I was; just one cup full made me a little sick and left me with a headache; maybe it didn't mix well with all the ice cream and bananas.

Johnny, with Shiva and his sister

Chapter 25
No Walking Today

For the first time in twenty two days, I was not able to walk.
The last time it was blisters that had stopped me; this time it
was the brain and common sense. After being advised by SV
and Naresh not to walk this part of the journey, the time had
come to face up to the dilemma.

I had discussed this issue with Johnny and after both of us
studying the map in great detail, we realised that following
SV's advice was the correct move. This was a big decision to
make and as soon as I had made it, I knew that I would never
really be able to claim that I had walked the whole way across
the whole of India following the Godavari River. In short, I
had failed. And I felt sad. I knew, even from the outset that it
wasn't possible to walk the whole distance, from one town with
accommodation to the next was, in some areas, impossible.
That point had also been highlighted by Prakash, the wine
farmer, who warned that sleeping in a tent was dangerous due
to the wild leopards. But in some way, I had forgiven myself
and when I abandoned the tent, I accepted the fact that I
would need to catch a ride between various locations. I had
accepted that as being alright, as long as I could still stick to
my goal of walking a certain number of kilometres each day.

What else could I do alone and unplanned? But not walking
at all was a different matter and this did not sit well with me.

The reasons for not walking were obvious, but for someone that was supposed to be crossing the whole of India on foot, I just didn't want to have to face up to. In the past, when I looked at this part of the journey, I had just ignored the problems it created; naively thinking I would find a solution. But I hadn't and no matter how long I mulled it over, I never would have. This point was then further hammered home to me by SV and Naresh; if I did actually attempt to walk this part of India, alone, unplanned and unguided, I would possibly never make it out of the other side alive.

There wasn't just one specific reason why it would be total madness to attempt to walk this part of the journey, there were several reasons that, when you combined them altogether, the honest truth was that it was not possible to do. I still was fighting with the naïve idea that everything is possible if you just have faith. So many times on this trip so far, faith had helped me on my journey, but to sum it up, it just wasn't possible, feasible or advisable to walk this part of the journey. The terrain was made up of thick, dense forest, with no villages or towns for miles (and miles). Even if I was mad enough to walk this and attempt to sleep by the side of the road, there was a serious issue with drinking water, or the lack of it. No population, no water. I was carrying water purifying tablets and even purifying straws, but nowhere to sleep combined with no access to clean drinking water; these two factors together were off putting.

.But this was not the only, nor the main reason, why walking through this particular area was not possible. The key reason, the one that was really worrying, was my safety and this was something in India that I had never had to worry about. That alone speaks volumes and is a credit, not only to this wonderful country, but more about its wonderful people. In this particular region, kidnappings and terrorist attacks were happening all the time. Some were reported, but many did not even get acknowledged. Two white men walking through a dense forest wearing ladies' hats, to say we might be a target would be putting it mildly.

It was a big all-round NO.

Making this big decision and choosing to not walk part of this journey, I realised that I would be finishing the trip earlier than I planned or estimated. I wasn't sure how I felt about that, but it did mean that I would have tell my wife and children - who were planning to jump on a plane from Mumbai and meet me at the end of the river, and the end of my walk, when the Godavari entered the sea and completed its full journey – and soon.

We had discussed this and they knew that they had to be flexible because I really had no idea how long this journey would take. Johnny consoled me with the decision that I had taken and deep down, was most probably thanking his lucky stars, because as much as he was enjoying the adventure, I am sure he couldn't wait to get back to Southport in one piece, recount his adventures, before watching Liverpool play. The fact that he wasn't mad enough to walk through a terrorist area could only be considered the normal thing to do.

One thing that did lighten the mood on this depressing day was the fact that pronunciation of the places and villages that we needed to get to had slowly become worse since Johnny had arrived. When I was on my own I realised that when I asked the various bus conductors to stop the bus at a village in the middle of nowhere, most simply didn't understand the name of the village I was saying, so I would write the name on a note pad and hope they could read the name and let me off in the correct place. But when Johnny was with me, listening to me trying to pronounce these names, he could not help but fall about laughing.

There was one small village that started with the letter 'T' that had at least fifteen letters in it, and when I attempted to pronounce it, the giggles started. In the end I just called it *Tombliboo*, after the characters from "In The Night Garden", the BBC children's TV programme. It is strange how such small and irrelevant things can make you laugh, and change the atmosphere from a worrying situation into a light-hearted one.

Rather dejected, we arrived at the bus station and made sure we were sitting on the correct bus. It was an unhappy time. I never planned to be sitting on a bus, watching the rural countryside pass me by and having no chance of being out there, walking through it. But as we drove on, it was quickly obvious to both of us that we had made the correct decision. Hours upon long, tedious hours of dense forest, starved of human life for the most part. An odd settlement appeared and vanished quickly every two hours, but nowhere along the side of the road was there anywhere to stop and buy water. In the middle of nowhere, the bus paused at what would struggle to be called a small town; there were no houses, just cone shaped straw huts.

The bus was already crowded and yet more people climbed on board and somehow were all squashed in. A women beggar got onto the bus and Johnny kindly gave her some small change.

Yet this somehow offended her and for the next hour, she would not leave him alone. She continued to pester him for more money, as obviously in her opinion, what he gave her was not enough. He eventually became angry with her, but she was also angry, becoming more aggressive. Her need was far greater than us two well-fed westerners could possibly imagine.

Despite the heat and lack of space, I feel asleep and regardless of Johnny saying that there was no way the he could sleep on such an uncomfortable bus, he also drifted off, sitting upright, holding on to a metal pole. The journey was not smooth and every time the bus hit a bump or crater in the road, Johnny's head hit the pole he was clinging to; yet still he slept on. It was not a pleasant journey. After ten long, uncomfortable hours, we were safely through the danger zone. It was a day I wanted to forget, and I couldn't wait to get back walking tomorrow. It was only one day, but this trip was about walking and we both missed it. After another night's sleep in another poor hotel, morning time came around again and we found ourselves waiting to leave on another bus.

This time I had planned it so that we could jump off at a temple and walk into the nearest town called Ashwaraopet, where we would be able to find accommodation. It was 5.45am before the bus arrived and my trousers were already soaked through with sweat, standing waiting in the station.

The bus took off and Johnny was asleep again. This time instead of continuously banging his head on the pole in front of him, he simply rested against it. It wasn't long into this journey on this crowded bus that I realised the bus was not going the way I had planned and was taking a totally different route. The road we were driving on was a single track, and there were holes everywhere. How Johnny managed to sleep through this trip was an amazing achievement. Like yesterday, there was not much sign of life out of the window, except for the odd tractor, but there were monkeys everywhere. There were so many of them that it almost felt like we were driving through a safari park. The scenery was different from yesterday; the forest was not as dense; it was beautiful. There was the odd straw coned hut and it would be true to say that this was the most rural part of India I had seen so far.

Continuing to drive through this countryside, the simple landscape on both sides of the bus became increasingly more impressive. All of a sudden, the bus came to a swift halt and everyone lurched forward. What on earth had happened? People were peering out of the window, jabbering loudly and pointing. Not wanting to miss out on whatever was out there causing all the excitement, Johnny and I strained our heads out of the window.

There, in the middle of the day, in the intense heat, was a gigantic snake. It was the biggest snake I had ever seen outside of a zoo. Green in colour, it made its way, slithering slowly, across the road. Johnny calculated that it was at least ten foot long, and he may have been correct. Even the locals appeared amazed seeing such a creature. It was the first snake that I had seen since starting the walk, and at one point, I was getting worried that I would complete the whole Indian experience and not see one.

Not long after the sighting of the snake, we got off the bus and start walking. Worries were piling up. Due to the bus's alternative route, the distance to our next stop had to be recalculated. We estimated that we had at least fifteen kilometres to walk; with the sun getting hotter by the minute, we had to increase our walking pace before the temperature became unbearable. Another worry was water and the lack of places to buy it.

With this in mind, Johnny and I were carrying over two litres infused with hydration salts each, so even if we were unable to buy water, we should still manage to walk the day's distance. The last of our worries was that we were now walking along the same road that we had just seen the enormous green snake, so we decided that the more noise we made as we walked the better.

Lots and lots of people were stopping, as always, on their bikes, in their cars and on their tractors, all offering their help. One cheerful man stopped his bike and spoke to us in English. Informing us that there was no water for sale along the main road, he luckily knew a village where we could get some. Johnny and I had now been walking for nearly three hours and we reckoned that we probably had enough water to make it to the next town, but we were getting low. Looking at each other and acknowledging our situation, before we knew it, both of us, along with our two large rucksacks and Raj, (for that was the man's name) were all on his bike, riding off the beaten track to find the village where we could buy water. In another place and time, this may have been considered a risk, especially not knowing this man who could be taking us anywhere, but this was India and, guess what... we trusted him, and guess what... we were glad we did.

True to his word, Raj, with all the weight on his poor bike, slowly transported us to the village. We spoke to him whilst driving along. He was completely overwhelmed meeting westerners near his home town and he kept repeating how lucky he felt that he was giving us a lift on his bike. He was swearing all the time, without realising it and he sounded like an America movie star. I would guess that his English had come from watching American movies and his accent was a mix between Bruce Willis from the *Die Hard Movies* and Robert De Niro, from *Taxi Driver*. Johnny and I struggled to hold back our laughter.

*'Hey man, I am so f***ing lucky to have met you guys, so f***ing lucky'.*

In no time at all, we were all standing outside one of Raj's friend's house and the whole village had turned out to see who Raj had transported to their home. Two strange looking white men: one very tall, one very short, both wearing ladies hats. This time Johnny was certainly the centre of attention. Everyone wanted to speak to him. I was just the old man that could have passed for his father, if my legs weren't as short as they are. Raj suggested leaving Johnny with the crowd and drove me further into the village where I bought water. Returning a few minutes later with the water, I couldn't even see Johnny. He had been completely swamped by the whole village. He loved his moment of fame, but afterwards admitted that as good as it felt, he couldn't bare the attention someone famous receives every day. I asked him why were they were more interested in him than me and he simply replied that he was better looking and younger. I chose not to reply.

We were now further off the beaten track and needed directions to put us back on the main road to the nearest town. He really wanted to take us further by bike but we refused. Thanking Raj, we left his village and continued to walk.

As we walked, more and more people were stopping and posing for selfies with us. Then a rickshaw stopped and five young girls got out of the back. Seeing women out in public was rare by itself; seeing young women out in public was even more unusual. They were completely fascinated by Johnny and obviously didn't give the old a man a second look. In fact, they only wanted to have Johnny in the selfies they took. I just stood by the side of the road and looked on. I realised that the wonders of youth had left me many years ago. Another hotel was found; another day was over.

Cone shaped dwellings

Chapter 26
Nashik to Yanum

'Why are you walking?'

'Where are you going?'

We were walking along the side of the road, trying to follow the path of the Godavari River, being stopped by fascinated people that wanted to help or take a selfie with two white strangers walking across India.

It got to the point where I was only explaining my mission to the people I thought would understand and, if time allowed, I took the time to talk in the sun when I really should have been walking. I would produce my golden ticket, written in Hindi that explained that I was walking for charity and to help the children I teach in the Mumbai slum. Then came the words that I had repeated many times:

'I am walking across India: Nashik to Yanum, started in Nashik and walking to Yanum'.

This would then have to be explained further. Lots of people were familiar with Nashik, as it was a large town and most could understand that was where I had started my journey. But Yanum? Not many people, especially in the rural centre of India, had ever heard of it. Yanum in Puducherry.

Some people then would have heard of Yanum and were amazed that I was trying to walk all the way from one side of India to the other.

Johnny had heard me say '*Nashik to Yanum*' so many times that when people stopped to ask what we were doing, it made him laugh. He said that I must have got so used to saying these two places, the start of my journey and the end of my journey, that maybe I should have named the book '*Nashik to Yanum*'. He also commented that I had got so used to saying the same words over the time had I had spent alone that I could no longer say them with using my hands to explain. He was so right and when he had pointed this out to me, I was very conscious of the fact my hands were moving. I would draw an imaginary map in the air. Start Nashik, finger pointing and finish Yanum, here. I would then say '*yes, all the way across the whole of India*'. I think I just liked to see the look on people's faces, as they just could not believe that I would be attempting such a distance. Further questions. Alone? Yes. Walking? Yes.

If I then explained that I was following the Godavari River, they then appeared to understand the course or path I was following.

Waking up early as usual, I was really angry to find that we were locked into the grounds of our hotel. I always make sure that when I booked a hotel, I tell them I will be leaving very early in the morning, 4.00am or 5.00am the latest. When we booked into this hotel, it did look as if there was no one on duty at reception, so I explained that I would need to get out of there early. The manager assured me that he would be around, and after thirty minutes of trying to climb a huge padlocked gate, we had to phone him. After a further wait of half an hour, he turned up. I gave him a piece of my mind and tried to explain that guests cannot be locked into a hotel, while the manager goes home to sleep. I further lost my temper saying what if there was a fire, how would we have escaped? I think the quickness of my speech and loudness of my voice was lost in translation. Johnny had to calm me down and after all I had experienced on this trip, I think this was the angriest I had been. When I look back on it, I know I totally over reacted, but I put that down to a build-up of frustration that I had kept to myself for all the day's walking I had achieved. But whatever way, the lock-in had made us late by nearly one and a half hours and after looking at the day's plan that could only mean more unbearable sun than we wanted to deal with.

But more important things were happening than being stuck in a hotel. Johnny was leaving India and this was his last day. The time he had spent with me had passed so quickly.

If Johnny was leaving, I realised that I must be getting close to finishing my journey. I had not wanted to think about finishing this marathon walk. I figured the more I dreamed about meeting my family on the last day, the slower that day would come. But the brain is a difficult thing to control when all you have to concentrate on is one foot in front of the other for hour upon hour, alone, with the sun beating down on you. But with Johnny's imminent departure, this really was the first time I had given serious thought to nearing the end of my quest.

After jumping yet another bus, and walking for another six hours, I was right in my planning - we were still walking in the mid-day sun and after experiencing this problem before, I knew it was dangerous. Johnny, just like I, was really struggling to cope with walking at this time of the day. Months later, when the walk was just a memory to share, I would look back, grateful that Johnny had experienced the struggle I had been through; yet now we both agreed that to be walking for too long at midday in this heat was utter madness.Finally arriving in the town, we found a hotel. We were both exhausted; our clothes completely soaked through to our underwear with sweat.

We struggled to find somewhere to eat. A man that took us to a restaurant, but it was closed; it really did look like the only place you could sit and eat in. After a promise of opening the restaurant for us, (which sadly, did not happen), we were both back on the streets searching for somewhere to eat.

It had been a difficult day's walking, coupled with the intense heat we now just needed to find food.

Deciding to sit down at the side of the road, we noticed a place that looked like it could be a café of some sort. Plastic chairs and Coke Cola signs were a good indication that we should be able to get something to eat. A man approached us, maybe in his 60's, who was the owner or a waiter and from this point on, the situation got worse. Firstly, there was the language problem, but I had got round that many times before and as long as we could get some rice and vegetable dhal, I would be happy. But as I sat on the plastic chair opposite Johnny, I could see he wasn't too sure that this was a good idea. There was no one else in sight except for this waiter man and that is never a good sign. I thought back to my green hospital where I had eaten with my hands and remembered whatever I ate, I was not alone; in fact, that particular eating establishment had been full. After only a few minutes, the waiter, who looked like he had not washed for weeks, came to the table carrying two silver plates with rice on them, banged them down and then added a jug of tap water.

As he put down the jug, I noticed the dirt under his finger nails and the grime on his palms. I really didn't think this was a good idea. I looked at Johnny. He looked as if he felt the same, but he didn't say a word.

Something in my peripheral vision startled me and I quickly turned around. I thought I had seen something move and jump into the sink at the back of the shack where this man had washed our tin plates. After leaving the jug of water on the table, he disappeared behind a wall, returning this time with the dhal, (or to be honest, green slop). Johnny looked at the food and was prepared to go along with my decision. After all, he knew no better and even though this was his last day of his journey, he guessed that I must have eaten like this many times before on my own and that this was a normal situation. But then again, out of the corner of my eye, I saw something black and hairy move behind me. Then it was gone.

Looking at the green slop, I said 'sorry Johnny, I can't eat here.'

I pushed the plastic chair back under the plastic table and got up and left. The waiter came running from the back of the shack and saying something angrily I didn't understand. But I was gone and Johnny followed me.

'That was close,' I said.

'Yeah, I would have eaten that but I am glad I didn't,' Johnny replied.

'Was it the slop that made you leave or just the fact that the waiter/cook was filthy?'

'Both of them, but when I saw that massive black rat, that was the final nail'.

'You idiot, J. That wasn't a rat, it was a cat!'

We laughed and thanked our luck stars that Johnny's last night was not spent being sick in the toilet. We walked on and luckily found some ice cream and bananas. Johnny's last night in India was spent safely in bed and not in the bathroom.

Sunset over rural India

Chapter 27
Johnny's Last Day

Up early and walking before the sun had come up. It was Johnny's last day before he left me and returned to England, and it was the first day for a while when we didn't have to catch a bus. We had fifteen kilometres to walk into Rajahmundry, where Johnny could catch a flight to Hyderabad and then a connecting one back to the UK. We had decided to end south of Rajahmundry, where we could cross the great Godavari before entering the town. Here, the river would be at its fullest and it seemed a very fitting way for Johnny to end his own personal expedition.

We walked for miles along the river's bank, seeing an immense bridge in the distance getting ever closer. That was our goal; to get to the bridge and let Johnny cross the river for the last time. It was unusual on this walk to be able to see a target you could aim for.

Normally, it was just a matter of following a road, or a path, to its end. Walking along the banks of the river, so early in the morning, we discovered that the local people used these banks as their toilet.

It was something that I had witnessed so many times in India that when I saw someone going about their morning routine, I didn't even turn my head. But for Johnny, it was his first experience of seeing another human being emptying their bowels in public for the whole world to see. He was shocked.

There were so many people crouching down it was difficult to find a path to walk on. The faces Johnny was pulling were funny to watch, and I had to fight hard not to laugh out loud. I think it was the smell that was making Johnny's face cringe. After seeing one person defecate in public, (male, I might add), then all and everyone seemed the same. We must have passed more than 15 people going about their toilet business. But one man we saw will forever be etched in my memory.

Crouching down with your bottom pointing outwards to make sure that your aim does not dirty your clothes is a definite art form. I have read that pooing, crouching down in this way, is more natural and better for our bodies. It is just us westerners that have become lazy, by sitting upright on the toilet. It is something that I have obviously had to master the best I could on this journey, with some, if not most places that I have stayed having only Indian-style toilets. However, I am still amazed how both feet and heels remain firmly on the floor when the action starts. I just have not got the flexibility to perform such an act.

This one particular man was going about his business with no embarrassment what so ever. Walking directly past him, he was in full flow.

Crouching down, he had a newspaper under his right armpit, and a hand rolled cigarette in his mouth. I don't know why, but seeing all these additions, that in some way can be loosely associated with men going to the toilet all around the world, made me think. Was this a working-class way people poo in India, or was I just thinking about this act more than I should have been? I looked at Johnny and Johnny looked back at me, with his nose in air, as if trying not to breathe or look in the direction of the man crouching down. But curiosity kills that cat, and for some sick reason, we both could not help but look. Then Johnny asked the question?

'Why is most of the poo we are seeing coming out of these men's bums yellow?'

To me, it was obvious. It was all the turmeric in their diet and I explained this to Johnny. There and then he learnt the dying capabilities of such a root spice.

Continuing to walk, our target bridge across the river was getting closer and closer. Approaching it, however, we both realised that it was a railway bridge and there was no way that we could cross the river this way. We were disappointed, but noticed that further in the distance, there was another bridge, so we continued to walk towards this.. We figured that the next bridge along must be a road bridge so Johnny's last day of walking had just got just that little bit longer.

After another hour of walking, we arrived at the road bridge and we knew that, finally, we could cross the great Godavari. Johnny had decided that this being his last walk, he would buy a wreath, from a man who was selling them at the side of the road. It must have been for a religious festival because even though the Godavari River was at its fullest, in no way, shape or form was this a tourist area. The wreath Johnny had bought was huge, mainly composed of different yellow flowers, all amazingly crafted together. He wore it around his neck (as if he had done this all before) and we climbed some steep steps at the side of the bridge that took us onto the considerable road that crossed the river. The road and the width of the river was 2.5 kilometres wide so Johnny and I agreed we were going to make sure we walked this last part of our day slowly, taking as many different pictures as we could, taking in all of what we were seeing.

It was a fast road over the bridge, being the main route in and out of Rajahmundry, but for once we were not aware of the speeding traffic or the enormous trucks that were rumbling past us; we were only interested in the river. There was a pavement so we felt safer than we normally did when walking along the side of such a busy road. The river really was incredible. Wherever you looked, no matter what direction you turned, you could see water.

In fact, it was so wide, it looked like the sea.

It felt good to be elevated up on the bridge so that you could experience in some small way the magnitude of it; it was, quite simply, vast. We both agreed that taking photos of it did not justify what we were experiencing and the fact that I had been following this river for weeks made the photographs even less significant. I told Johnny that when you see something as magnificent as this, you must try to take a photograph in your mind and keep it there. The last time I had taken such a mind photograph was when I first saw the Grand Canyon in the US, and even now after many, many years have elapsed, I still have that photograph stored safely in the back of my memory. This was one of those occasions where words and photographs were not as valuable as the memory itself. This seemed like the perfect point for Johnny to gift his wreath into the river and he ceremoniously threw it off the bridge. It spun and as we were so high up, we didn't see it land. But we imagined it floating on the water and drifting down stream in the direction I still had to walk.

It took us an hour to cross the river and it is something that neither of us will ever forget. This was the last time Johnny would be seeing her and he vowed that he would come back and see her again one day.

We both had fallen deeply in love with this river. Johnny was leaving, but I still had her company right to the end of her, and my, journey.

We had decided that if we could walk to the bus station, I could find a hotel for the night and Johnny would have a good chance of finding transport to the airport. Johnny did his last bit of walking and the hotel that I booked into managed to find a taxi for him to drive him to the airport. We said our goodbyes in the reception of the hotel, and the manager of the hotel took a picture of us both, where again, the height difference between us both made everyone laugh. I knew I would miss him. I had really enjoyed his company over the last five days; we had been so lucky to experience together all the things that had happened. He had kept me young, and at times, made me feel old.

Waving him off as he got into the taxi, I was alone again. How did I feel? Firstly, I had a similar feeling to that I had when I had started out with the entire width of India in front of me. Me, and me alone, versus the road again. But, for the first time with Johnny gone, I began to think that I could see the winning post. For the first time, I could hear myself saying 'keep your eyes on the prize.' It wouldn't be long until I could see my family again. I had missed them so much. I could now allow myself to think of a proper bath and warm shower, clean clothes, a real non-vegetarian western meal, a beer and a non-aching body.

But even though I allowed myself to think of such luxuries, I still had a few days of walking ahead of me.

SV phoned me to see how I was doing, and was extremely pleased to hear that I had taken his advice and not walked through the forest and dangerous terrorist areas. I assured him that having taken his advice (and even though my trip had been cut short), I was still alive to tell the tale. We both laughed and with Johnny gone, I felt that SV was looking over me. After I had stopped speaking to him, that same niggling thought I had when I was in his company washed over me again. A thought that I couldn't put my finger on, but for some reason and even though we shared laughter, I could sense that something big was worrying my friend. I wished I knew what it was or I had the courage to ask him.

*The wreath disappears into the
Godavari River*

Chapter 28
KSR: The Water Wallah

I felt strong today, the strongest I had felt for ages. My feet were blister free and it had taken nearly thirty days of walking before they had become used to what I put them through on a daily basis. How ironic. Just as I was coming to the end of my trip, my feet felt good. I had decided to try and walk more than twenty kilometres today, and that was something that I hadn't really been able to achieve all the way through this journey so far. When I started out on this trip, I discussed the length of a decent daily walk with a good friend of mine who told me that to walk twenty kilometres every day was a real achievement, especially if you are doing the same amount one day after another, and he was so right. He knew this because he had completed the *Camino de Santiago,* the walking pilgrimage through northern Spain.

After walking for a few hours, with the heat taking its toll as usual, a rickshaw stopped. A man got out and I thought it was just going to be a quick selfie and then back to the walk ahead. I looked in the back of the rickshaw and it was full of empty crates and there was no space at all on the seat.

On the front seat next to this driver was an enormous container, a twenty litre water container. We tried to communicate and what I could understand that this man, whose name was KSR, (obviously another name that was easily abbreviated just like SV to make it easy for me to say, and thus making it easier for us to get along). He was, in fact, selling the water along the side of this long stretch of road to anyone who would buy it. What a genius idea. It was not the first time since I starting this trip that I had been amazed by the way people think and act to earn money. Inventing a job to make money to survive. I thought back to when I stayed with Sarang, and the time his car had a flat battery, two men showed up and, pardon the pun, charged Sarang 100 rupees to get him going again. KSR gave me a few free glasses of water and drove off. Even though this was a long road, in some ways, it felt more touristy than anywhere else I had walked so far. Maybe it was because I was approaching the coast. However, saying that, other than Johnny, I had still not seen another white face so far. Another two hours of walking slowly ticked by along the same road, and KSR returned. He stopped me again and explained that he had removed all the crates from the back of the rickshaw, so now he could give me a lift to where ever I wanted to go. I tried to explain that I did not want a lift and that I was walking, but he really did not understand. Then, from the back of the rickshaw, under the seat where the crates had once been stored, he produced a huge yellowed flowered wreath, not dissimilar to the one Johnny had bought to walk over the river. He then blessed me and wrapped the floral wreath around my neck. It was a lovely gesture and yet again, I was blown away by the friendliness shown to me by a stranger. I was a guest in his country and walking on his water patch, his road, and he wanted to show me how welcome I was. I knew I had a problem and that there was no way that I could walk another ten kilometres with this large wreath around my neck, because after putting my rucksack on, it was practically choking me. But I saw the happiness on his face when he gave it to me, so there I was, standing next to him and his rickshaw full of clean water, thinking how I could get out of this situation without offending him. One, I couldn't take the wreath off and two, I did not want a lift in his rickshaw. Pouring me yet another cold clean glass of his merchandise, we smiled. Not wanting to offend this man, I kept the wreath around my neck and jumped into the back of his vehicle, remembering it was the experience and the adventure I was after, not just the walking. But I explained that I could only travel with him one kilometre further down the road.

He accepted and I think he understood after I produced the golden ticket, explaining that I needed to walk.
We took some photographs, exchanged numbers, and I left him travelling back up the road we had just come down in the hope of selling some more water. And the wreath? Well, I left on the back seat of his rickshaw, hoping he didn't see it, and hoping I had not offended him.

It wasn't long before I had reached the town Mandapeta. This was my second-to-last day and I didn't want spend a long time looking for a hotel. I just wanted to get to bed and make sure I was fresh for my final day's walking. I found somewhere dirty and overpriced, but that did not bother me. I could see the winning post now and nothing was going to dampen my spirits.

KSR, the water wallah

Chapter 29
Sandgrounder

The plan was set: meet the family and together, we all walk the last five kilometres of my journey. Sounds easy, but it would be all down to the timing. Michelle and the boys had flown out to meet me and were spending the night in Rajahmundry as it would have been too late to meet up that evening. I was spending my last night in a place called Ramachandrapuram and we had planned to meet in Yanam, my final destination.

I was not sure how I felt when I woke up. Was I sad that this trip was coming to an end, or was I happy that, regardless of how, I had been able to get to this point? I had only one more walk to complete before I reached my final destination. It had been a terrible last night. The hotel was awful and the noise of people talking and enjoying themselves kept me awake for most of the night. When I got up at 4.00am, I certainly was not feeling my best. But now I was working on nervous energy and I was so much looking forward to seeing my family again that one night's missed sleep was not going to keep me down. After a one kilometre walk to the bus station, I caught the 5.30am bus into Yanam. I had worked out that I had almost three hours walking before I met the family. My last walk alone and I didn't really know what I was expecting. But, like most things that have happened to me on this journey, it was amazing.

I had decided to take a path that would let me walk the closest I could in order to follow the Godavari on the last stretch of its journey into the Bay of Bengal. Here the river and I had something in common: we were both coming to the end of our long journey.

After leaving the bus behind and really not wanting to see another Indian bus ever again, I had a bit of a spring in my step. I was walking again. I thought I would feel the same emotions I had been experiencing over the last few days walking alone, for hours on end. But I really didn't feel that way at all. I was just determined to concentrate on the moment and enjoy the present. This was the end and I was going to enjoy every last moment. As I walked, I cast my mind back and tried to think about when I began this journey. It seemed so long ago that it felt like a distant memory. It was only my diary and blogs that I had written en route that would later transport me back into a moment that I could relive. Again, I took a phone call from Habil, the lorry driver, just hoping that I would make it back to Mumbai in one piece. I realised that this man had called me every single day since I had met him. I also heard from SV, who was over the moon that I was safe and had made it to the last leg of my journey.

I walked along speaking to him, but there was something still bothering me. I could sense that there was something important he wanted to tell me, but I suppose he figured that as I walked my last walk, this was my moment and whatever he wanted to tell me, he could tell me when I had finished this journey when I was safely back with my family in Mumbai.

I walked through Yanam and I was really impressed by how clean it was compared to most of the towns I had walked through. People were just going about their morning routines of brushing their teeth and emptying their bowels on the streets, turmeric included. Soon I was walking beside the great river, and I could not help feeling a bit sad and overwhelmed, just like when Johnny said goodbye to the Godavari. It had been my shining star that I had followed over these many weeks and the saddest thing was, after spending so much time following it, I felt sad because after I had finished this trip, I was not sure when I would see her again. If ever.

People were working on the river, and working hard. They were dredging sand from the bottom of the river and filling their boats to such a point it was unbelievable that they were still afloat. Shiva, (a friend I had met a few days ago), told me that the collecting of this sand was totally illegal. I am not sure if this was true or not, but these people certainly didn't seem at least bit shy, or embarrassed by what they were doing.

I had a thought and wondered what damage collecting this amount of sand could be causing the river. But this was big business and with the amount of cement this country uses, sand is a necessity. I met more locals and a man on a motor bike followed me along the path and got me to take photographs of every sandgrounder that I passed; the workers enjoyed posing for the camera; all smiles and cheers as I clicked away. These men were wearing nothing except their under pants and a towel wrapped around their heads. This was heavy work, not just dredging the sand, but also carrying it to the shore. As I experienced these last moments, the boats that were collecting the sand continued to defy science and remained afloat, despite being so low in the water. The path that ran beside the river suddenly just stopped and the only path that I could take took me away from the river and headed towards a distant village. Like many times before on this trip, I just took the path really having no idea where it would take me.

This really was an ironic moment and nicely summed up the way this wonderful adventure had gone. I was taking this last path in hope of meeting my family soon, but it was not following the river as planned. Just like this whole walk, I had started out following the river the best I could, but had soon come to realise that it was not going to be possible to follow it all the way; I had to continue my journey another way, different to the way I had imagined.

But none of that really mattered; it was the adventure, the unknown that had made this so memorable for me. Not the route, not the miles I had covered. If I had followed the river all the way by foot, who knows what would have happened. But the fact was I had not. I really did not know where or what way I would travel across this country. This uncertainty, for me, made this a continuous, unknown adventure and that was so much more enjoyable. Making this quest come alive was all the people that I had met along the way. So now a path I knew nothing about once again took me away from my river. Yet there must have been a reason for it. I wanted to spend the whole of my last day on the banks of the Godavari River, and here I was walking away from it. So what, I thought, I still had the rest of the day to say goodbye to her.

Turning away from the river, I thought if I headed towards the village, there might be a main road that would lead me down to the meeting place. It would be here that I had decided would be a good place to walk to with my family. But I still had to meet them.

I came to a mass of open land, and here I saw children playing cricket. They called me over. I was going to decline my last game of cricket purely because of the time and the scheduled meeting. But I could not resist a quick bat and bowl. Right arm over, spin, with the rucksack still on my back.

A young boy played and missed; the ball just missed his off stump; the crowd groaned. Then it was my turn to bat, and I stroked the ball through the covers but I did not run – the rucksack was too heavy.

I could have easily walked past these children, or if I had tried to follow the river along its banks, never come across them at all. That would have been really sad, and this last game of cricket I played with these children would be remembered for a long time, whereas another day's walking along a road, or a river, could soon be forgotten. It was all about the people I had met, and I was still meeting, all the way to the finish line. When I had bad times and good times and even now, it was the people that made the difference.

I soon found the road and had to walk quickly to make up time. I was meeting the family who were travelling by car to join me. I spoke to Michelle on the phone and we arranged to see each other at a petrol garage near a jetty, on the banks of the Godavari. The timing was slightly out and the car carrying all of them pulled up alongside me. I told them to continue on and I would meet them at the garage. Their driver really could not understand what was going on. But it just would not have worked, stopping the car on a single-track road, all hugging and kissing each other. I walked on to the garage and finally, we all embraced.

But the walk had to continue to its end and we all still had over an hour of walking to complete. But not without a dip in the water first. I had had many opportunities to swim in the great river and each time, I turned it down, wanting to save this for the end of the walk. The jetty I had in mind was not ideal, but this would be my only chance. My two boys and myself stripped down and got ready to enter the water. We were in a small fishing community and with five minutes, word had got around and soon we had around thirty boys and men watching us in amazement. The water was not too clean and the mud on the bottom felt like sinking sand, but we still took the plunge. I could have stayed in the water for a lot longer. I had made it. I was swimming in the great Godavari River that was about to end its journey and flow into the sea.

After a change of clothes, we were soon back walking. Andrew, my oldest son, was not feeling too well and walking in this heat was really not doing him much good at all. The driver that Michelle had paid to be with us all day just followed us as we walked along. I felt that at last and, for the first time, I had a guide. I felt like someone famous as the driver slowly drove behind us as we walked the last few kilometres to the end. A few people passed and wondered what was happening, but how would they really know how I felt inside. The driver just thought we were all stark raving mad!

The walk was to finish at a landmark called *The Obelisk Tower* in Yanam. This was the place I had tried to picture in my mind for weeks. The words *'Nashik to Yanam'* would never need to be repeated again. At the tower, it was possible to climb up a hundred metres and see the Godavari River flowing effortlessly into the sea. The Tower also happened to be a smaller replica of the Eiffel Tower in France; but this tower was in the middle of nowhere. It felt a bit soulless, but for me it was not the middle of nowhere. It was the end.

I thought about this moment: the one I had dreamed of time and time again as I walked the miles; I thought it would be an emotional time. In a way it was and being here with the family, it could not help but be somewhat poignant. But if I had to describe this feeling, this emotion, I would describe it as a *mixed* feeling. Even though I tried to live in the moment, I could not help but think back to what I had accomplished. I had walked 584 kilometres in total over thirty one days. I wasn't sure if this was a great achievement or not. It certainly was not the 1465 kilometres, the length of the Godavari River, I had first planned. I was experiencing what all great explorers feel when they finish their quest: to the top of the mountain; the end of their walk, it does not matter what the final goal is. It was coming to an end and I could not help feeling both happy but, at the same time, sad. It was not about the achievement now – it was about what I would be missing. The unknown, the adventure, all this would stop now. But I did not want it to.

The trip was over; my walking had finished. But the memories I had gained from this adventure would live on and the people that I had met would, I hope, remain my friends for many years to come.

Reunited with the family once again

Epilogue

The last thing that I wrote in my diary when I finished the walk was about my re-entering the western world again. A world full of money, of property and greed. In lots of ways, these were things that I hadn't missed at all.

Life moved on and soon I found myself, along with my family, leaving India behind to start teaching in a different country. In fact, I went on to teach in the Bahamas, and that could not have proved to be more different from the Indian world I had left behind. I still stayed in contact with most of the people I had met during my walk, mainly through the marvels of modern society - social media. The one person that I spoke to on a weekly basis was my good friend SV.

When I explained that I had decided to leave India, he appeared really upset, and I don't think he really could understand why. He would say, after all that you have achieved and all those children that you had helped in the Mumbai slum, why would you want to leave? I don't think he could ever understand that I felt what I had done had been completed.

I felt that I could have stayed on in India and worked more to help the children that I was teaching in the slum. But after the walk and raising the money, nothing else I did would ever match up to that. I felt that it was time to move on. I obviously had considered my children's education and my wife also felt that a move from India would be a good thing. I felt so strongly about my time here in India that I wanted to leave on a high. If I had stayed, then what was to follow could never match up to what I had just achieved. I wanted to leave India with a feeling that had me longing to come back. I couldn't explain all these feelings to SV over the phone or via social media; the language barrier between us was too big for him to understand my logic.

Each week he would send me photographs of himself either working in his cement office or just sitting on his bike. He would send me photographs of us two and the short time we had spent together. There was still a sense that he was not telling me everything that was going on his life and still I never plucked up the courage to probe any further.As I adjusted to my new life in the Bahamas, SV would continue to contact me as if I was still in India, or if I was just around the corner. He was worried about a young boy in his neighbourhood, who had lost his mother years ago, and just recently his father had been taken ill and was dying. He sent me pictures of this young man and asked if I could help in any way.

He never asked me to send over money, just if I could help. I tried to explain that even though I had just walked across India and raised money for children that I was teaching in Mumbai, there were thousands of people that I would like to help, but I simply could not. SV did not see it like that. He saw me coming into his life as a person who would help people just like he would and now, perhaps, we could now help people together. When I explained that I was sure that he could help, living in this man's neighbourhood whereas I was living in a different country, hundreds of miles away, which meant that I could not, I think he was disappointed. That was the impression I got. However, despite my being unable to help, our strange and wonderful relationship did not change. He would ask my advice on all sorts of things and I would share my thoughts with him. I would ask him for his advice because it was due to SV that I had started to meditate. He had opened a new world to me, and despite reading all the books on meditation I could get my hands on, he was still my guru. One morning, I got a message from him.

He was extremely worried and sounded like he was in shock. I was teaching at the time, so I told him to calm down and that I would contact him when I had finished teaching.

But before I had the chance to phone him back, he had already sent me photographs of himself. He had been involved in a motorbike accident. He explained that he had been knocked off his motorbike by a lorry and that he was lucky to be alive. I was shocked and he had spent a few days in hospital recovering; he sent me pictures of himself covered in blood, wearing a badly wrapped bandage around his head. He explained that he was not sure if they could save the two fingers that had been badly injured during the accident. I tried asking how such an accident had happened and how his fingers had got so badly hurt, and not his hands or arms. He was very vague with his answers and did not explain what happened at all, except that a lorry had run over him and his motorbike. I was in shock and naturally, very worried, but the fact that he was safe stopped me asking for further details. I suppose being badly hurt was a bit embarrassing for him and he did not want to talk about it. Not for the first time, I was not really sure that SV was telling me the whole truth. But soon he was back to himself and he was lucky that both his fingers could be saved.

He then started to send me more photographs of himself, showing slowly how he was recovering from his accident. I was pleased and soon we were back to normal. He never mentioned the young man that he had wanted me to help again, and I would still pick his brains to the many and varied methods of meditation.

Leaving to go to school one morning, I looked at my phone, and what I saw left me stunned. I had received a graphic picture message from an Indian number that was not in my contacts address book. It was a photograph taken from a newspaper article of a man lying on the floor, blood oozing from his head. The blood was a vivid red. Lying next to the man's head was a rock, also covered in blood. I looked at it and I was shaken. It was 5.00am my time and I was just waking up; I was completely taken aback by this. Who would be sending me a picture of someone lying on the floor, blood trickling out of their head? I wasn't sure, but when you see such an unexpected, disturbing picture like that, you don't know quite what to think, but whoever it was that was lying on the floor looked like a dead man. I had to wake up Michelle and she agreed that whoever that was on the floor, he was most definitely dead.

Looking closely at the attached article, we agreed that it was written in Hindi. This confirmed my initial thought that this had something to do with someone I had known in India. Someone who need me to see this distressing image. I cannot read Hindi and the print was far too small to see details, such as a name, to explain who this poor man could be. The face of the man in the photograph was covered in so much blood that it did not look familiar at all.

I knew that I would have to speak to whoever had sent such a shocking message. The time difference was such that I would have to wait until lunch time to attempt to phone.

Shaking when I made the call, deep down in the back of my mind, knowing who this man was, I was just hoping, praying that I was wrong. But my worst fears were confirmed when Naresh answered the phone, and before he could complete his first sentence, I knew SV was dead.

For the first few minutes of the call I was not really listening to Naresh, SV's best friend, the man that had done my washing for me using only his feet. Naresh was crying as he spoke and it was not long before I was joined him. I explained that I had only spoken to SV just two days previously and he was fine. What had happened? But Naresh could only repeat the same phrase over and over again:

'John Sir, SV is dead'.

'What happened to him?' I asked, tears filling my eyes.

'He was murdered by his wife and her brother. She is not a very nice person, and I told you that John'. I really did not know what to say to Naresh. I desperately wanted to find out more. Really? His wife had murdered him? I realised that whatever questions I asked Naresh, to find out what had happened to SV, did not matter.

The reality was that I would never speak to him again. I had lost a friend. I had a sick feeling in my stomach. I was angry, annoyed and sad all at the same time. I needed to know why his wife would kill him; such a placid man, a religious man, a man who had an inner peace with himself and everyone he met. A meditator and a mentor to many.

Quizzing Naresh over what had happened to SV, he just replied that it was over money. His wife was not a very nice person. I knew it had to be more than that, I knew that there was something when I first met SV that I could not explain to myself. But, to be murdered? It was all too much to take in over the telephone. I thought that maybe it had been about the properties that SV had said he owned and told me that he needed to sell.

All these thoughts were running around my head. Were the properties bought with his wife's family money, and that was why he needed to sell them? Was this all to do with his time in the Middle East, that he did not want to talk about?
So many questions were in my thoughts, questions that I would still be asking years later, and without a trip back to India and hiring investigators, questions that, sadly, I would never find the answers to.

This frustrated me. 'Naresh, I spoke to him only two days ago, I had no idea that he was in trouble with his wife'. 'John Sir, I had no idea either. His wife is not a nice person'. 'He recovered from that accident a few weeks ago, when a lorry run him over'. 'John Sir, that was no accident'.

The phone went quiet again. The accident had obviously not been an accident and his wife, along with her brother, had tried to kill him before and failed. But this time they had not failed, and he had been hit several times on the back on the head, in his own street, with a large rock and had been left to bleed to death.

As Naresh explained the final act in gruesome detail, a deep feeling of sadness washed over me. Naresh was doing his best to explain to me what he thought had happened, going on to say that the police now had the wife and brother in jail, and that they would not be released any time soon.

To kill your own husband by bashing him on the head with a rock shows such untold signs of hatred that I could not even begin to comprehend. I said that I was no longer able to take all of this in and thanked Naresh for phoning me and letting me know. He knew that in only a short time, SV and I had struck up such a good friendship.

A week passed and I phoned Naresh for an update. He explained that the funeral was taking place that day, and again we both cried together. SV had touched my soul and I would never forget him. When he had offered me a copy of his family's photograph the day I met him, I wished now that I had taken it. But I do not need anything tangible to remember him by and every time I mediate, I think of my good friend, SV. Rest in peace my friend.

Weeks passed and I continued getting on with my life, and the terrible act that had happened to SV in India faded. I had calmed down; I would continue to miss him and remained disappointed that our friendship would not develop any further. But I had come to a peace with the way he had been murdered, and after trying to work out what I thought the reasons for such a terrible act might have been, I had accepted that I would never know and if truth be told, I really did not want to know.

SV's death just would not go away, though. I thought about it a lot, when I was on my own and my wife and I had discussed it over and over again, trying to reason what would have driven his wife to commit such a heinous crime. Then, two weeks after the funeral, Naresh phoned me.

'John Sir,' it's Naresh'.
'Hi Naresh, how are you?'
'SV is dead ..... You are my friend now. Forget SV, he is dead'.

I just looked at the phone and I was shocked by the frankness of Naresh's attitude; I really did not know what to say. He continued:

'Next time you come to India, forget SV. He is dead. I am now your friend. You will come and stay with me and my family and be a guest in my house. You are my friend now SV is gone'. Upset at first by Naresh's attitude, I think that what he had meant was lost in translation. I found that like many Indian people I have met, he had a very practical way of dealing with death. They just accept it and move on. That is all he was saying: SV has gone, let's not get held up on the past, and try to change something that we can't change. Let's move on.

But for me, that was difficult. From all the wonderful people I had been lucky enough to have met, SV and his attitude to life would stay with me forever. I did not want to forget him. I know I could not change the fact that he was no longer with us. I did not want to be angry that his wife had killed him. I would never really know why, and I did not want to know why. But the fact that I had been lucky enough to have met him and spent a whole day and night sleeping on the floor next to him, would never be forgotten, and I never want it to be.

The death of SV just highlighted what this mission, or adventure, had turned out to be. Forget all the miles I had covered walking. Forget all the physical pain and blistered feet

I had to treat.

Forget all the wonderful places I had visited and, even forget the great Godavari River, which really would be the hardest of all to forget. Forget everything, because the people who read this story would have realised that this was an adventure about meeting people. I had forgotten over the years that meeting people is what happens when you travel. I had forgotten that if you take yourself out of your comfort zone, it is the people that help you and that is what this adventure was all about. All those wonderful people that had gone out of their way to help me, advise me and encourage me to reach my goal.

When I look back in ten years' time, it will not be the fact I had swum in the Godavari, nor that I had seen the sun rise over rural India nor that I had walked the whole width of an amazing country that I will remember.
It will be all those marvellous people, exemplified by SV that will remain in my memories forever.

My friend, SV

No-one became poor by giving

It was time to give. I had walked the walk and talked the talk. Now I needed to give. The money I had collected from people's kind donations would be put to good use. I had decided that I would buy all the resources for the slum school myself and deliver them in person. That way, I could decide what to buy, and being a teacher, I knew which resources would best benefit the children I had been teaching. The other reason was that I knew that all the money raised would be used directly for the slum children's education, and not be lost or used within the charity's system. The remaining money I collected for the *Brian Tumour Charity* I planned to give personally to my friend Mat Bayfield, when I next returned to the UK.

After buying all the books, I had not given a single thought to the way I was going to deliver them to the slum. I needed help, so decided to take my two sons out of school for the day to help me.

There on the floor of my lounge were all the resources I had bought for the school. Even with help, and riding by taxi, instead of taking the train, it was going to take two visits to deliver it all.

The first day, I took Andrew, my eldest son, and we ordered a taxi to take us to the slum to meet Isobel, the teacher I had been teaching with the most. Andrew was excited about going to slum to see what it was like, to meet all the children and the teachers I had spoken about over the time we had been in India. He had had to put up with all my stories; now he was going to see for himself and form his own opinions.

Sadly, when we arrived at the school, the children had not returned from their summer break, so we only met Isobel. She was amazed by how many books there were and was astonished that Andrew and I had managed to carry them all.

I had to tell her that I would not be coming back to work on the slum after the end of June, and we both shed a tear. She quickly said that it was not goodbye and that our paths would cross again. I have found a lot of Indians would say this and I liked it, and with the time and experiences I have had, I am sure that I will be back. Who knows, it might even be to promote my book about the walk.

We did not stay for long, and knowing I would be coming back for another book drop off, made the fact that I was leaving India easier for us all to handle.
I asked Isobel when the children would be coming back into school, and she told me that it would be the next day. We left with me telling her I'd be back then.

On the second visit to the slum school the following day, I used the muscle power of my youngest son, Theo, to help me as well. This time, although we had more books to deliver, we also had all of our no longer needed clothes for Isobel to pass onto to children in the slum. Included as well were boxes of Lego and K'nex that the boys had out grown, duvets, quilts and anything else useful that we were not shipping on to our next post.

Taking another taxi, and afterwards, a rickshaw and train home, the boys loved the trip. The driver of the taxi was amazed by the amount of items we had squeezed into his car. He was also really curious as to why we were going to slum, and I had to explain that I was a voluntary teacher there. This time, arriving at the slum, laden with bags, the children were in class, learning. After removing our shoes, we entered Isobel's classroom, and all the children stood up and welcomed us. My two boys just could not believe the amount of respect shown to us. Soon Andrew and Theo were sitting on the floor with the children and helping them with their work. Some of the newly delivered resources were already being used, and again, this brought a tear to my eye.

We then walked over to the other side of the slum to deliver all the resources that I had bought for my other class. I would not have been able to have transport all these resources without the help of my two sons. Walking across the slum, people were staring at us, carrying all these books, but the boys just smiled and followed me to the other classroom.

Here, just like with Isobel, the children all stood up and welcomed us into their classroom. The teacher, Sanchita, was speechless when she saw all the resources we had ready for them. The children had drawn me a picture with words of thanks on the back.

Soon, the boys were helping the children learn, joining in with a game called 'Fire in the Mountain', where the children run around in a circle and the teacher sings 'fire in the mountain, run, run, run.' A number is called out and the children group themselves according to that number. Lots of pushing and laughter, Andrew and Theo were enjoying themselves. One 6-year-old girl would not let Andrew go and just kept looking up at him. He was double her size; it made me feel like laughing and crying at the same time.

The morning session finished with everyone standing up, singing Jana Gana Mana, the Indian National Anthem. We all joined in, I almost knew it!

We walked back across the slum back to Isobel's class, and the boys met some more of the teachers. I promised that I would come back next week for the final time, even though I still had not packed all our items ready to be shipped. The boys loved it so much they asked if they could come back next week as well, and hopefully, I was planning to bring Michelle to share in this moment: it had been such a big part of my life whilst living in India. I wanted my whole family to come and meet all the children and teachers of such a wonderful place - a Mumbai Slum.

As the title of this chapter says, *giving never makes you poor*. I would say it does a lot more than that. By giving my time and experience freely to these people, I have been the one that has received.

I will never, ever forget my experience here and I feel blessed to have been given the chance to teach in a Mumbai slum. I really do hope one day I can come back.

I will never, ever forget my experience here and I feel blessed to have been given the chance to teach in a Mumbai slum. I really do hope that one day I can come back.

My task is complete.

==============

Isobel with her class and Theo, with the books purchased through the sponsorship of my walk through khush India

'Everyone should have a chance to take part in an adventure during their lifetime. Whatever shape or form that the adventure turns out to be.'

Acknowledgments

There are so many people I would like to thank for making *Walking Khush India* possible. I just hope I have not forgotten anyone.

My brother Steven, for agreeing to look after my car while I was away, and phoning whilst I was walking. To all my friends who phoned me whilst I was walking, in particular John Larkin and Jeff Andrews, who just by speaking to me kept me going and made me determined to reach the end. To Sange Wilson, for looking after our two lovely cats when we moved to India. For all the people who sponsored the walk and donated money for the books and resources that were bought for the slum school in Mumbai. To Suffolk Radio, for interviewing me and making my trip known to the public. To Matt Bayfield, (who, sadly is no longer with us) for his support, guidance and advice on raising money for good causes. Also, for his inspiration in showing the importance of walking for getting people together and promoting the benefits of walking.

Ange Larkin, Mavis Jones and Dorothy Turner for their help in ordering all the equipment I needed for the walk. And to Angela Castro Rodriguez, in Ortigueira, Spain, for helping me purchase the tent that I never got to use!

To the doctors and anyone who gave me advice on walking, including my Spanish friend, Antionio Barba.

To all the schools and children in the UK that followed my blog and supported my cause from start to finish.

To the two charities, *Door Step School Mumbai* and *The BrainTumour Charity,* for all their support and guidance in fund raising.

To my school colleagues, Denise Clark, for her help and advice in preparing the book covers; Sarah Bain, for all her help and advice completing the front cover and back cover of the book. She is the one who drew the wonderful sketch, the map and the drawing that I felt made the book come to life.

To my good friend Richard Smith, for all his help, before, during and after the trip. Both he and his wife, Lorraine, gave me help with organising fund raising, advice during the walk, particularly on how to deal with constant blisters; for his phone calls whilst I was walking to keep me focused and keep me laughing, when at times I wanted to give up and cry; and for his help in editing the book and help organising the layout and publishing of the book.

For Josie Howard's help and advice in editing the book and to her son, Johnny Ball, for his companionship during the walk and the conversations that kept me sane.

And to all the people who followed my blog and sponsored my charities.

Inside India

With many thanks to *Door Step Schools*: the teachers, Isobel, Sanchita and Ujwala.   To all the people working at the paper making factory, Athulya in Munnar, Kerela, that provides work for the physically challenged people. I bought a book there and all the workers signed the cover. I used this for my diary of the walk: it is made from elephant dung and recycled paper. To LB, (or, as he is really named, Iaxmikant Deshmukh); Sarang Savil; Lata Salvi; Sanket Salvi; Lukrie Salvi, and Sharad Tukaram Chapke.To all the people in the village of Katneshwar; Sachin Harichandra Chapke; Kamal Kishanaro Jadhav (Sharad's grandmother), Ram Chapke Patil; Habil; Dr. Lohiya Rajest; the Dentist; the ox cart driver; to the kind village lady who gave me chai; Rushikesh Dhokane Patil; Robert Raj, my driver at the start of the walk; Asif Monde; the machinist who sowed my rucksack and trousers back together; Satis, Satis and his daughter; Kausar and his friend Prekash and his family; Tasher Tarle; Decpali Tushar Tarle; Akshada; Agagv; Shashikant Tarle; Shantabgee; to Asif with whom I drunk chai with; all the teachers, and children I met in the schools I visited; Munna Lanke; Vinayak Sabbani Rao – or SV as he is known throughout this book (sadly, no longer with us); Gosikonda Naresh, the army man, who fed me and whose wedding I just missed; Pup the dog; Omprakash Dhage, the guy who gave me his sun glasses; a carpenter who found me accommodation.

Vijay; the students who picked me up and took me to the Social Security Office; the guys who helped me order a meal in the green hospital; Shiva; Raj; Prinz Arbanz; KSR and Ravi, the farmer.

To all the hundreds of people that stopped and offered help; all the people that helped me with directions and accommodation; all the bus conductors and bus drivers who stopped their buses in the middle of nowhere and allowed me to get off.

To anyone that might have helped me anyway.

To my two sons, Andrew and Theo, who would phone me, (or I would phone them), giving me the up-to-date football news and speak to me about things that would keep my mind off of the walking.

And finally, to my wife Michelle, for first making the trip possible by making me move to India; for her support and encouragement during the walk; for her financial support funding this trip while I was not working; for all her help after the walking, editing and organising the layout of the book. Without all of her help, this book would never had happened - thank you.

References:

1. Gregg Brown, East Anglia Daily Times (24-02-2018)
   https://www.eadt.co.uk/news/suffolk-teacher-john-massey-to-treck-across-india-for-door-step-schools-and-the-brain-tumour-charity-1-5408388

2. www.britannica.com/place/Godavari-River

3. research.net/publication/332142496, www.animalresearch.info

4. http://www.walkthroughindia.com/walkthroughs/top-5-largest-dam-of-maharashtra/

5. Shanti Project: *www.project-shanti.de*

Information:

Godavari Riverside Temples:
http://www.southreport.com/temples-at-godavari/

Printed in Great Britain
by Amazon